University of Michigan Business School Management Series

INNOVATIVE SOLUTIONS TO THE PRESSING PROBLEMS OF BUSINESS

The mission of the University of Michigan Business School Management Series is to provide accessible, practical, and cutting-edge solutions to the most critical challenges facing businesspeople today. The UMBS Management Series provides concepts and tools for people who seek to make a significant difference in their organizations. Drawing on the research and experience of faculty at the University of Michigan Business School, the books are written to stretch thinking while providing practical, focused, and innovative solutions to the pressing problems of business.

Also available in the UMBS series:

Becoming a Better Value Creator, by Anjan V. Thakor

Achieving Success Through Social Capital, by Wayne Baker

Improving Customer Satisfaction, Loyalty, and Profit,
by Michael D. Johnson and Anders Gustafsson

The Compensation Solutions, by John E. Tropman

Strategic Interviewing, by Richaurd Camp, Mary Vielhaber,
and Jack L. Simonetti

Creating the Multicultural Organization, by Taylor Cox

Getting Results, by Clinton O. Longenecker and
Jack L. Simonetti

For additional information on any of these titles or future
titles in the series, visit www.umbsbooks.com.

Executive Summary

To be successful in today's fast-paced business environment, organizations need the knowledge, ideas, energy, and creativity of every employee—from those at the front line to those in the executive suite. The best companies create within themselves a *company of leaders*—an organization in which employees at every level take initiative and act as owners of the firm.

How does a company transform its workforce into a company of leaders? By creating an environment in which people are empowered to bring their whole person to their work. Yes, *empowered*. Although empowerment has gone out of fashion since it first became a buzzword in the 1990s, the problem is not with the essential concept but with the way it has been misunderstood and misapplied. This book draws on a decade of empirical research to show how employee empowerment, properly understood, can transform a workforce of followers into a company of leaders.

To uncover the fundamental kernels of truth embedded within the idea of empowerment, Chapter One applies a "controlled burn" to the construct to remove misunderstandings and evolve the concept into a robust and practical approach to unleashing the real power within your employees. Drawing on extensive research in many kinds of companies, the chapter shows that genuine empowerment is not something that managers or the organization "do" to employees. Rather, empowerment reflects a set of expectations on the part of each individual that encompasses a sense of meaning, competence, self-determination, and impact. The task for managers and organizations is to create the conditions that foster this choice to be empowered.

Creating the right conditions for empowered behavior requires commitment, dedication, self-control, regular attention, practice, sacrifice, and practical know-how. Chapter Two crystallizes these ideas into the five disciplines of empowerment. The chapter explains how sustaining a climate of genuine empowerment requires balancing the tensions among seemingly contradictory disciplines, for example, vision and challenge versus security and safety. The *continuous* and evolving practice of all five disciplines is necessary to stimulate the kind of creative tension that fosters leadership at all levels of the organization.

The next five chapters focus on the individual disciplines. The first discipline, *self-empowerment,* is discussed in Chapter Three. This discipline sets the stage for the others by focusing on the self, because only empowered leaders can develop an empowered workforce. The chapter provides an assessment to benchmark your own level of empowerment and suggests avenues for personal leadership development.

The other four disciplines describe the key elements of an empowering system. Chapter Four focuses on the discipline of *vision and challenge.* Inspiring and aligning people to the organization and its mission provides the personal connection necessary for empowered behavior. Chapter Five describes the complementary discipline of *support and security.* Resources, training, a reward system focused on individual and organizational performance, and a culture that encourages learning are some of the steps required for creating the psychological safety so necessary for people to feel comfortable in taking on the risk of leadership.

Chapter Six describes the fourth discipline, *openness and trust*. This discipline creates an atmosphere that entices real employee involvement in the organization. Its complement is the discipline of *guidance and control,* presented in Chapter Seven. This discipline is about creating the boundaries and structures necessary to assure the empowered behavior stays on track. Chapter Eight offers an assessment tool for evaluating the state of all five disciplines in your organization and summarizes the steps managers and executives can take to strengthen those disciplines that most need improvement.

Throughout the book, real organizational examples illustrate the disciplines of empowerment, and specific tools, techniques, and strategies are presented so that committed readers can put the disciplines to work. The end result is an organization where employees at all levels take initiative, act innovatively, engage in transformational change, and act as though they are owners. What could be a more effective source of competitive advantage?

A Company of Leaders

Five Disciplines for Unleashing the Power in Your Workforce

Gretchen M. Spreitzer
and Robert E. Quinn

JOSSEY-BASS
A Wiley Company
San Francisco

Published by

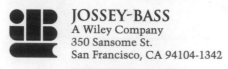

JOSSEY-BASS
A Wiley Company
350 Sansome St.
San Francisco, CA 94104-1342

www.josseybass.com

Jossey-Bass books and products are available through most bookstores. To contact Jossey-Bass directly, call (888) 378-2537, fax to (800) 605-2665, or visit our website at www.josseybass.com.

Substantial discounts on bulk quantities of Jossey-Bass books are available to cor-porations, professional associations, and other organizations. For details and dis-count information, contact the special sales department at Jossey-Bass.

Credit lines are on page 199.

We at Jossey-Bass strive to use the most environmentally sensitive paper stocks avail-able to us. Our publications are printed on acid-free recycled stock whenever possible, and our paper always meets or exceeds minimum GPO and EPA requirements.

Library of Congress Cataloging-in-Publication Data

Spreitzer, Gretchen M.
 A company of leaders: five disciplines for unleashing the power in your workforce/
Gretchen M. Spreitzer and Robert E. Quinn.
  p. cm.—(University of Michigan Business School management series)
 Includes bibliographical references and index.
 ISBN 0-7879-5583-3 (alk. paper)
 1. Leadership. 2. Employee empowerment. 3. Teams in the workplace. I. Quinn, Robert E. II. Title. III. Series.

HD57.7 .S699 2001
658.4'092—dc21

2001032676

FIRST EDITION
HB Printing   10 9 8 7 6 5 4 3 2 1

Contents

With love to our spouses
Robert Schoeni and Delsa Quinn

Series Foreword

Welcome to the University of Michigan Business School Management Series. The books in this series address the most urgent problems facing business today. The series is part of a larger initiative at The University of Michigan Business School (UMBS) that ties together a range of efforts to create and share knowledge through conferences, survey research, interactive and distance training, print publications, and new media

It is just this type of broad-based initiative that sparked my love affair with UMBS in 1984. From the day I arrived I was enamored with the quality of the research, the quality of the MBA program, and the quality of the Executive Education Center. Here was a business school committed to new lines of research, new ways of teaching, and the practical application of ideas. It was a place where innovative thinking could result in tangible outcomes.

The UMBS Management Series is one very important outcome, and it has an interesting history. It turns out that every year five thousand participants in our executive program fill out a marketing survey in which they write statements indicating the most important problems they face. One day Lucy Chin, one of our administrators, handed me a document containing all these statements. A content analysis of the data resulted in a list of forty-five pressing problems. The topics ranged from growing a company to managing personal stress. The list covered a wide territory, and I started to see its potential. People in organizations tend to be driven by a very traditional set of problems, but the solutions evolve. I went to my friends at Jossey-Bass to discuss a publishing project. The discussion eventually grew into the University of Michigan Business School Management Series—Innovative Solutions to the Pressing Problems of Business.

The books are independent of each other, but collectively they create a comprehensive set of management tools that cut across all the functional areas of business—from strategy to human resources to finance, accounting, and operations. They draw on the interdisciplinary research of the Michigan faculty. Yet each book is written so a serious manager can read it quickly and act immediately. I think you will find that they are books that will make a significant difference to you and your organization.

Robert E. Quinn, Consulting Editor
M.E. Tracy Distinguished Professor
University of Michigan Business School

Preface

I magine for moment a company where employees at all levels take initiative without prodding, where every employee
acts in the collective interest of the organization without
being monitored. In short, imagine for a moment what it would
mean to have a company of leaders. What a competitive advantage such a company would have in today's competitive business environment!

This book is a step-by-step guide to creating this kind of organization. Such a company is not a pipe dream. We have seen
companies create success by tapping the capacity of leadership
inherent in their workforce so that employees contribute all they
can to the firm's success.

How do these companies create leadership throughout the
organization? They do it by creating an environment in which
people are empowered to bring their whole person to their work.
Yes, *empowered*. We almost hesitate to use this term because the
notion of "empowerment" has been so misunderstood and mis-
used since it first became widely popular in the 1990s that many
businesspeople have all but given up on empowerment as a way
to transform the workforce. Yet ten years of empirical research

have shown us that, properly understood, empowerment is necessary for creating a company of leaders. To discard what was true and valuable in the concept of empowerment is to throw the baby out with the bath water. A more useful response is to learn from both research and experience—to arrive at a better understanding of empowerment, avoid the mistakes of the past, and discover how to create competitive advantage by unleashing the power in your workforce.

Based on our research, we take the notion of empowerment through what we call a *controlled burn* to remove misunderstandings and evolve the concept into a robust and practical approach to getting the most out of your employees. Genuine empowerment, we have found, is not something that managers or the organization can "do" to employees. Rather, it is a set of expectations on the part of each individual that encompasses a sense of meaning, competence, self-determination, and impact. With this mindset, employees become *self*-empowered. The task for managers and organizations is to create the conditions that foster the choice to be empowered.

The payoff? Our research shows that empowered employees take initiative, are innovative, engage in transformational change, and are seen to be highly effective. In short, they act as leaders. A number of examples in this book illustrate how this kind of shared leadership can take an organization to new heights.

An empowering environment also brings important benefits to employees. Empowered employees are more committed and satisfied. They find their work more interesting and meaningful. They feel challenged to learn and grow to their full potential. This is the kind of work environment that can make an organization the employer of choice for talented workers.

Such results can only be achieved through a thorough understanding of what it takes to create an empowering environment and the dedication to see the effort through. In this book, we introduce the five disciplines of empowerment—the sets of practices that are necessary for encouraging employees to align themselves with the collective purpose and to make spontaneous contributions on its behalf. One of the keys to putting these disciplines into practice is to recognize that there is a creative tension among them. Empowerment isn't just about vision and challenge; it's about providing security and support. It isn't just about openness and trust; it's also about guidance and adequate control. Most important, empowerment isn't just about organizational structures and processes; it's about empowering *oneself*. Taken together, the disciplines encompass the tensions and paradoxes inherent in empowerment.

Who can benefit from mastering these disciplines? The short answer is anyone who wants to develop the leader within and who wants to contribute to creating a work environment where leaders can develop at any level. More specifically, in our teaching, consulting, and executive education courses, we have found the message of this book to speak to a range of individuals, including the following:

- New managers who are just learning how to coach and inspire their people
- Experienced managers who want to reinvigorate their direct reports to take initiative and grow
- Human resource managers who want specific ideas on how to create organizational systems and policies that grow leaders throughout the organization
- Organizational development specialists who seek innovative approaches for bringing culture change
- Executives in organizations that have been through painful restructurings and downsizings who are looking for ways to rejuvenate their people and systems

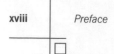
- Small business owners looking for strategies for creating ownership throughout their ranks

A word of warning, though: This book isn't about quick fixes and magic bullets. The disciplines of empowerment are just that—disciplines that require commitment, dedication, practice, hard work, and persistence. This book provides the understanding and the tools; the rest is up to you.

■ Acknowledgments

We thank our many colleagues, clients, friends, and students who have helped us over the past ten years as we have shaped our ideas and conducted our research. The Michigan Business School and Marshall School of Business provided important resources and release time for the research reported in this book. We gained particular insight from the intellectual horsepower of these colleagues and writing partners: Susan Ashford, Jean Bartunek, Warren Bennis, Susan Cohen, Jay Conger, Tom Cummings, Jane Dutton, David Finegold, Ed Lawler, Gerry Ledford, Aneil Mishra, Neil Sendelbach, Ken Thomas, and Karl Weick. We are grateful for the constructive feedback we received on selected chapters from our reviewers, Tom Helton of United Stationers Supply Company, Bradley L. Kirkman of the University of North Carolina at Greensboro, and Aneil Mishra of Wake Forest University. We also thank Kimberly Hopkins Perttula for her editorial assistance.

We would like to thank the Jossey-Bass team, especially Cedric Crocker, Byron Schneider, and Kathe Sweeney, for their support of this series and our ideas. They were instrumental in framing the manuscript. We are particularly grateful to John Bergez of Bergez & Woodward for his masterful developmental editing and brilliant suggestions, particularly the suggestions that helped us find the right title for this book.

Most important, we thank both our families (including Claire Englishby). It is from them that we have learned what genuine empowerment is all about. They have created the environment that nurtures and challenges us to be what we are.

May 2001

Gretchen M. Spreitzer
Los Angeles, California

Robert E. Quinn
Ann Arbor, Michigan

A Company of Leaders

Unleashing the Power in Your Workforce

T his is a book about creating a company of leaders—a workplace where people at all levels are energized to contribute as much as they can to realizing the organization's goals; a workplace where people at all levels show initiative, flexibility, and innovation in their everyday work and decision making; a workplace where people at all levels are as committed as any executive to making the organization successful. Our goal is to show how you can change your behavior and your organization to unleash this kind of power in your workforce.

In this book, we will demonstrate that creating a company of leaders requires empowered leadership. From our years of research and practice, we now know that empowerment comes from within, not from administrative programs. Empowered leadership begins with you. It requires you to take a hard look at yourself to see whether you are modeling the very mindset and behavior you seek from your people. Such empowered leadership must then be complemented with a special kind of work environment where your people will be stirred to take initiative to further the collective purpose of the organization. This kind of environment leads to increased commitment and spontaneous contributions on behalf of the organization. Creating this kind of empowered leadership and environment requires what we refer to as the *disciplines* of empowerment—the disciplines that allow you to unleash the power within your workforce and create a company of leaders.

Does a company of leaders sound too good to be true? We maintain that this kind of organization is not only possible, it is essential for competitive advantage in today's marketplace. Consider the following two examples of truly high-performing workplaces.

■ Too Good to Be True? Just Ask These Companies

Our first example comes from some work we did recently with a well-known pharmaceutical company. The example begins as we relay our experience with their top management team.

As we started our session together, our colleague asked the top management team to make a list of the strengths of the company. They did. As the list grew, and despite my initially positive feeling, we began to suspect that they were posturing. The list was too good to be true. The characteristics were outside the normalized realm of organization. Consider their claims:

- We are proactive: When a product is still climbing in the market, we move on.

- We shape practices in the market.
- We love responding to a challenge.
- We think big and seek success at all costs.
- We are the place you go in the larger corporation if you want to become a leader.
- We cannot stand to be anything less than number 1.
- We take strength from having done the impossible in past crises.
- We are highly galvanized and rally in times of crisis.
- We have quality people with a "can-do" spirit.
- We have people-friendly policies; it is a place of high trust.
- We appear to have very few formal systems, but when a problem arises, a team spontaneously emerges, solves it, and then disappears.

The last statement seems to be the most extreme claim of all. At the moment it was made, a woman on the management team responded: "That is right. I have been here three months, and it is driving me crazy. I have worked in a number of corporations, and I pride myself on being able to rapidly comprehend the culture of any organization. This place baffles me. I watch those teams form and disintegrate. It is like magic. I cannot understand or explain it."

To this statement, there was a rejoinder by another member of the organization: "I have been here more than a year. I am in charge of systems and processes. I cannot understand it either. It is an extraordinary phenomenon."

As the day unfolded, we became convinced that the list was for real. These were people with a powerful culture. The company was a productive community. It was a hard-driving organization making lots of money. There are, however, many hard-driving organizations that make money. This one was more. It was an organization in which people were as committed to each other's success as they were to their own. Because there was trust, people could communicate their problems, get help, and cooperate. The self-interest, which is the bedrock of most corporate cultures, was also operating here, but the collective interest and individual interests were one. Here everyone was a servant to the system and to each other. This was a focused, money-making company that was also a productive community.[1]

Our second example comes from an interview we conducted with a senior executive of a *Fortune* 500 company in the building industry. The executive managed branches all over the world. He told us the following story:

Our worst branch was in Detroit. On every numerical indicator they were at the bottom. We could not find anyone inside who would head up that job. I had an application on my desk from a guy who had been fired by one of our competitors. I kept telling myself to throw it out but I kept picking it up and rereading it. Finally I called the guy. There was something about him that appealed to me. He knew who he was. Anyway I took a risk and hired him. That was eighteen months ago. Today that branch leads the company on every major indicator. When I visit I see the same bodies that were there before. But now there are different people in those bodies. They are full of fire. You feel it when you first walk in. You know you are in a world-class operation. People are focused, they walk around with a sense of intention. They care about the customer. They care about each other. They are enjoying themselves while they produce the best numbers in the corporation. When I leave I feel like I want to be better. It is difficult to define what it is, but I will tell you it is a contagious thing. I try to visit them as often as I can.

These two stories are cases of people and organizations living up to their potential. If the stories seem extreme, it is only because they illustrate something that does not happen in most organizations. In the first story, members of the organization are highly energized. They willingly take initiative. They work together in spontaneous ways that seem almost magical. They have a workforce of people willing to take initiative—a company of leaders. The second story is very similar. What is striking in this story is that the organization was once at a dreadful level of performance. But something happened. Employees across the organization were enticed to reach their full potential. They began to behave like leaders.

In these kinds of companies, people do their best work because they *want* to. Their minds and hearts are intertwined with their work. Just as important, they show initiative, they take responsibility, and they are innovative and creative. Their power to contribute is unleashed.

There are many ways we might characterize the employees in our examples. We could say they are energized or vitalized. We could say, in a metaphor that has become popular in Silicon Valley, that they act almost like volunteer employees—people who contribute their best effort willingly, not because they have to earn a living but because they want to. Or we could say, to use another popular image, that they act as though they were owners of the firm. We think the best way to characterize these kinds of employees is to say they act like leaders.

■ Why a Company of Leaders Matters

Although the attractiveness of a workforce that behaves like leaders may seem obvious, it is worth considering the many reasons that creating a company of leaders is a competitive advantage. Indeed, in the business world of the twenty-first century, a company of leaders is arguably a necessity. In today's marketplace, many products and services are becoming commodities. Where products and services offered by competitors are seen as interchangeable, the level of service and responsiveness distinguishes one company from another. And that means that what employees do and say matters more than ever before. Given their proximity to the customer, lower-level employees can often spot problems better than upper-level managers. They are the ones who endure the customer tirades resulting from a bad service policy and the ones who spot product defects as they go out the door. And they are the ones who can solve those problems if they have the power and willingness to act.

Further, increasing competition, a global economy, and rapid technological change require organizations to innovate continually in order to survive. The kind of passive obedience that worked when it was sufficient to do the same thing over and over efficiently won't take today's organizations where they need to go. To be competitive in today's fast-changing environment, organizations need the knowledge, ideas, energy, and creativity of every employee, from the front line to the executive suite. A successful organization requires the flexibility and innovation to respond to rapidly changing market and technological conditions. Like innovation, flexibility needs to be both a mindset and a lived reality throughout the organization.

The flattening of organizational structures creates another reason a company of leaders is essential in today's business environment. With whole bands of middle managers removed in white collar downsizings, employees are expected to be more self-managing. More and more often, employees work in self-managing teams that make all the decisions pertinent to their work, including hiring, firing, and disciplining their members— behaviors that have long been the responsibility of leaders in the company. In a flat organizational structure, leaders are necessary at all levels of the organization.

For all these reasons, today's challenge is to create an organizational culture in which all employees want to work to their full potential—to take initiative and act as an owner of the firm. Yet this challenge arises at the very moment when it may be harder than ever before to attract, develop, and retain people with the skills, motivation, and dedication to behave like leaders. Record low unemployment rates and a shortage of skilled workers has created a "war" for talent. High-potential employees are in extremely high demand, thus creating much competition among companies trying to attract them.

Hence, a company that can create a culture that attracts and keeps the best and the brightest would have an important competitive advantage. To be competitive, today's organizations need to create a culture that supports, nurtures, and develops workers to be all that they can be. Employees want to know that they are valued and that the company is investing in them to help them be all that they can be. High-potential workers demand such a work setting, and they are reluctant to leave it once they experience it. They know they will be unsatisfied and unfulfilled in a more ordinary environment.

■ How Can I Create a Company of Leaders? Revisiting a Familiar Concept

Over the decades there have been many attempts to describe how to create the innovative, responsible, dedicated workforce that every company should want. Veteran managers have lived through a number of "movements," including employee involvement, participation, and quality of work life. For much of the 1990s, the popular notion was "empowerment." We believe that empowerment has come and gone, not because it lacked value, but because it was incompletely understood and, to say the least, imperfectly applied. We believe that embedded in the notion of empowerment are important kernels of truth about how to energize and unleash the power in people.

In this book our aim is to draw out those kernels of truth and translate them into the specific behaviors that enable executives and managers to create a setting in which employees at all levels display responsible leadership. We do this by drawing on over ten years of rigorous research on the notion of psychological empowerment in the workplace, as well as a decade of experience helping organizations unleash the power in their workforce. Our belief is that there is still no better way to encourage employees to act like leaders than through genuine empowerment. But so many misunderstandings—and disappointments—have accumulated around the word *empowerment* that we must first make clear what we mean by *genuine* empowerment. We begin by doing a "controlled burn" of current understandings of this much-maligned notion, with the aim of disengaging the baggage that has accumulated over the years.

■ A Controlled Burn of the Notion of Empowerment

Over time, a forest accumulates a significant amount of debris made up of leaves, branches, and scrap trees. This debris sucks the life out of a healthy forest and can turn an ordinary forest fire in an uncontrollable inferno that devastates the entire forest. Many forestry ecologists believe that the way to prevent out-of-control fires is a process of regular controlled burns. A controlled burn is a premeditated fire or an unplanned fire from lightning that is allowed to burn off forest debris in a systematic manner. It is a quick burning fire that stays low to the ground. As a result, its flames do not reach the treetops, and tree roots remain undamaged. A controlled burn not only contributes to a healthy ecosystem but also creates something new: Some kinds of seeds can only be germinated when a fire breaks through their hard outer coating. So from the fire comes new life.

It is time to bring a controlled burn to the notion of empowerment. The idea of empowerment has become weighted down with significant baggage—or debris—that has sucked the life out of the construct. What happened to sour so many managers on the once-promising idea of empowerment?

The Promise of Empowerment

Empowerment's beginnings were in the civil and women's rights movements of the turbulent 1960s. The initial idea was noble: to give people the power to control their own destiny. For business organizations, transferring real power or decision-making authority so employees could control their destiny was more than most managers could stomach, so empowerment got translated into limited delegation and participative decision making. The hope was to get greater productivity from employees often with less management. During the 1990s, empowerment took on almost fad proportions when Peter Block's 1991 book *The Empowered Manager* became a management bestseller. Everyone wanted to say that they were "doing" empowerment.

As with many management fads, the core concept of empowerment was soon prostituted. Managers, consultants, and union members were implementing programs in the name of empowerment that had little to do with the genuine article. And when empowerment programs failed to work, people tended to conclude, "We have tried empowerment and it did not work."

Why Empowerment Failed

Our research suggests that there are five factors that particularly explain the failure of empowerment: (1) ambivalence, (2) bureaucratic culture, (3) conflict within the organization, (4) personal time constraints, and (5) a fundamental misunderstanding of how empowerment is achieved. Examining these sources of failure will help clear away some of the debris around the notion of empowerment and make room for a better understanding of how to release the power in employees.

Ambivalence
Empowerment programs often aren't really about empowerment at all. Genuine empowerment requires that authority figures become leaders of people, have the courage to give up control, and trust in their people to do the right thing. Many efforts at empowerment have failed because of a fundamental ambivalence about trading authority for empowering leadership.

When thinking in the abstract or about ourselves, most of us are quite comfortable with notions of initiative, risk, personal growth, and trust. We become much less comfortable, however, in thinking about these same characteristics when considering how we manage our own direct reports. We wonder about how much autonomy our people can handle without becoming loose cannons. We worry about losing control. When we measure our value by the authority we wield, we are likely to feel threatened by empowerment. Peter Kizilos has nicely captured this ambivalence:

> How lovely to have energetic, dedicated workers who always seize initiative (but only when appropriate), who enjoy taking risks (but never risky ones), who volunteer their ideas (but only brilliant ones), who solve problems on their own (but make no mistakes), who aren't afraid to speak their minds (but never ruffle any feathers), who always give their very best to the company (but ask no unpleasant questions about what the company is giving back). How nice it would be in short to empower workers without actually giving them any power.[2]

The reality is that many managers reinforce control systems that, intentionally or unintentionally, send the message that employees are not trusted to show initiative, take risks, or make responsible decisions. For example, organizations often develop such strict standard operating procedures that there is no opportunity for employee initiative when it is really needed to solve a customer complaint. Consider the case of an airline employee who went the extra mile to help reroute a frequent flier during a snowstorm and then was reprimanded because the policy for weather delays was not followed. You can bet this employee would hesitate to take initiative the next time such an opportunity arose.

These kinds of control systems create pressures for conformity rather than encouraging initiative and risk taking. When this happens, employees are apt to believe that an empowerment program is merely a guise to have them take on greater responsibility and assume more risks without additional rewards—and with an increased chance of being blamed when things go wrong.

Bureaucratic Culture

A bureaucratic culture encompasses multiple layers of hierarchy that inevitably impede change. In such a culture, to get an initiative approved, five people must say yes, but to get it stopped, only one of the five has to say no. This tendency is only magnified by a strong tradition of top-down direction and control. Typically the result is short-term managerial thinking, narrowly defined accountabilities, and lack of support for employee-initiated change. Further, the entire culture is reinforced by a reward system that emphasizes the status quo. Employees are rewarded for their performance in a given year rather than how they develop and grow the business for the future. In short, a bureaucratic culture creates barriers to change, risk taking, and initiative.

Conflict

Conflict at a number of levels—both up and down the hierarchy and across functions and work groups—is embedded in most large organizations. Often, for example, the organizational structure exacerbates the natural tension between functional areas by creating strong divisions between functions; some organizations actually refer to this divisional structure as "chimneys." The performance management system creates conflict between peers by pitting them against each other for raises and promotions, thus creating competition rather than collaboration. Not least, conflict between managers and subordinates over the means to achieve goals creates a hostile working environment where people worry about protecting themselves rather than doing what is right for the organization. Each of these sources of conflict discourages employees from taking initiative and focusing on doing the right thing.

Personal Time Constraints

Intense time constraints are imposed on managers and employees alike in the majority of organizations. In today's business world, with the trend toward downsizing and layoffs, one person may be doing the job of two or even three people. This situation actually argues for encouraging even greater initiative on the part of employees, but going beyond the routine takes time and energy. For example, management at the now defunct Montgomery Ward told salesclerks that they were "empowered" to accept merchandise returns that previously were under the authority of department managers.[3] At the same time, management cut staff and reduced benefits. The message was, We want more for less. Needless to say, employees didn't feel empowered at all. In addition, employees today often complain about having less and less time for family life. Working under these types of stressful conditions, people often indicate that it is very difficult to think about initiating anything new. If we want employees to exercise their initiative and discretion, we need to align roles, responsibilities, and work demands in a way that makes it possible for them to do so.

Fundamental Misunderstanding

A fundamental misunderstanding of how empowerment is achieved is reflected in a semantic trap that is all too easy to fall into: We speak of managers or organizations "empowering" their employees. In reality, it is clear from our experience and our research that no one in an organization can truly empower anyone else. *Telling* people they are empowered only demonstrates that the listeners don't really have power at all—that the authority figure is still very much in control. In short, most empowerment programs have been implemented so as to achieve the exact opposite of their espoused intent.

What managers and organizations *can* do is create environments in which people are more likely to choose to empower themselves. From the organization's point of view, it's less accurate and helpful to think in terms of "empowering" the workforce than to think in terms of *releasing* the power *in* the workforce to help the organization excel. When conditions are right, employees will indeed *feel* empowered—that is, they will feel trusted to make decisions, take initiative, be flexible, and do the right thing. As a result, they will be more likely to demonstrate the kinds of leadership behaviors that result in exemplary performance.

■ The Four Dimensions of Genuine Empowerment

Given the several reasons for the failure of empowerment programs, it is little wonder that the construct of empowerment has little meaning to so many managers. Yet all along there were important kernels of truth in the notion that empowerment can release the energy that creates real ownership and initiative in employees. Now that we have all been singed by experience, the task is to burn away the misunderstandings about empowerment, learn from our failures, and build on what was true and valuable in the original concept.

To begin, we need to come to a clearer understanding of what empowerment is. Our research suggests that genuine empowerment consists of *fundamental personal beliefs that employees have about their role in relation to the organization.* This view of empowerment emerged from in-depth interviews in which we asked individuals to describe times when they felt particularly empowered and times when they felt particularly disempowered. The resulting perspective was confirmed by our analysis of extensive survey data from a range of organizations.

More specifically, our statistical analyses reveal that the mindset of people who feel empowered has four dimensions: empowered individuals see themselves as having freedom and discretion *(self-determination)*, as having a personal connection to the organization *(meaning)*, as confident about their abilities *(competence)*, and as able to make a difference in the system in which they are embedded *(impact)*. Let's briefly examine each of these four dimensions as illustrated in Figure 1.1.

Self-Determination

Self-determination refers to the degree to which people are free to choose how to do their work. This dimension is close in meaning to popular perspectives on empowerment focusing on

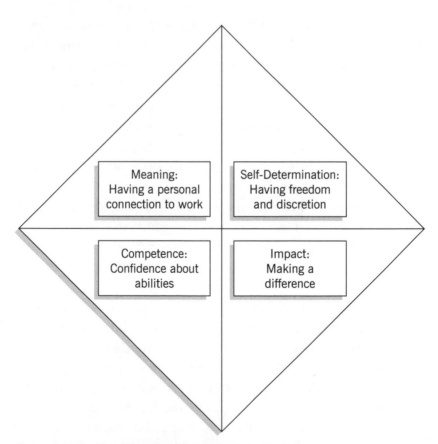

Figure 1.1. The Four Dimensions of an Empowered Mindset

delegation—giving individuals the power to make decisions. When people feel a sense of self-determination, they do not feel micromanaged. They believe they have the freedom to make appropriate decisions and take initiative when they see that something can be changed and improved upon. Initiative aimed at the collective good envelops the accountability and responsibility that follow from this kind of autonomy. A sense of self-determination is driven by a self-perception that one's involvement in a given activity is volitional and intentional rather than pressured and coerced by the larger system. Self-determination represents an inner endorsement of one's actions, a sense that they emanate from oneself and are one's own.

Employees in different organizations have expressed in a variety of ways the take-charge mentality of people who have a sense of self-determination:

- "With the help of my people, we decided the best way to attack [the problem]. It was our baby. It wasn't 'do it the way we tell you.' Instead, it was 'how do you think we should approach this?' "
- "I take things in my own hands. I am the one in the driver's seat."
- "I initiate action and am proactive. I decide what I think is the best course of action and then act on it. I take initiative at my own accord."
- "I am energized and free to decide the best way to get my job done. I feel autonomous."

Employees' feelings of self-determination are often cited as a primary reason for Southwest Airlines' (SWA) incredible safety record. SWA management allows pilots much more discretion in the cockpit than other airlines, which tend to rely on the autopilot and standardized procedures for virtually all segments of the flight, including takeoffs and landings. The upshot is that SWA pilots are engaged. The result is a spotless, nearly three-decade safety record.[4]

This kind of self-determination is becoming more of an expectation in today's business environment. More than ever people desire and enjoy having the authority to define their work, have personal control, and take ownership of what they are doing. Clearly, this dimension of self-determination is the foundation of a leadership mindset.

Meaning

Meaning is the degree to which people care about their work and feel that it is important to them. Employees feel a sense of meaning when an activity counts in their own value system—when they believe in what they do and feel that what they do matters. As one executive put it, the challenge is to move from success to significance—to create a sense of legacy, of some lasting presence. Involvement in activities where personal meaning is lacking can create feelings of dissonance and lead to personal disengagement. The result is work done by rote, without conviction. Conversely, activities infused with personal meaning create a sense of purpose, passion, and energy.

Meaning can come from either the activity itself or the outcomes associated with the activity, such as valued rewards. Whatever its source, a sense of meaning is the engine of genuine empowerment. Empowered individuals derive a sense of self-identity and personal integrity from their work. That personal connection with their activities energizes them to do their best work. These feelings are captured in the following statements by employees:

- "I was so excited about what I was doing that I couldn't wait to get out of bed in the morning—you know that feeling? My work took on a personal dimension that I don't usually feel. It really meant something to me."
- "Following those things and ideas that I think are important and necessary. It's working toward a personal vision of how

I believe that things are supposed to be. It means doing the right thing."
- "I am doing things that I most believe in and maintain my integrity."

Statements like these reflect the deep sense of meaning and purpose experienced by empowered employees. Many speak of the spiritual nature of the experience. There is a strong affective quality to these reports; people say that their "heart and soul" are into it.

Yet in the workplace, many people often feel a disconnect between their values and their behaviors. Living with that gap means that they are living in conflict with themselves. When people feel a deep sense of meaning in their work, that conflict disappears, and they feel a wholeness. They experience congruence among their values, their behaviors, and the organization's expectations. This wholeness is reflected in one entrepreneur's response to his personal physician, who asked how many hours a week he was working. The entrepreneur replied, "I don't know. How many hours a week do you breathe? It's one integrated whole." This is the essence of personal meaning in work.

Competence

Empowered people are confident about their ability to do their work well. Individuals feel confident when they have the ability and technical *competence* necessary to perform a task *and* that no outside causes will prevent them from attaining the required level of performance. Here are some statements from employees that express feelings of competence:

- "As a woman, I always felt that I had to prove myself. I wasn't always very confident about what I had to contribute. But doing [the project], I felt extremely confident in myself— I knew that I did have what it takes, that I could do it and do it well."

- "I know I have the skills and abilities necessary to get a project done. It's feeling confident, believing in myself, trusting myself, knowing that I can do it. I can follow my intuition."
- "[My job was] highly challenging, but never completely beyond my capacities. I was able to overcome especially difficult times on my own by drawing on my special talents and abilities."

In addition to feeling competent to perform familiar tasks, when people are empowered, they believe in their capacity to learn and grow to meet new challenges. They have a sense of personal mastery. As an example of what can happen when a sense of competence is lacking, listen to this story told by a high-ranking executive about his arrival at an Internet start-up:[5]

> After just two weeks, my boss asked me to present a product plan to my colleagues. I was shocked. He tried to reassure me: "Just throw some slides together and tell us what you want to do." The rest of the company was only about fifty people. I came from a big conglomerate where the idea of figuring out a new product, let along presenting it, took months or years. I had no idea what to do; needless to say, the meeting went badly. My voice tends to quaver in direct proportion to the amount of bull in my message—I was virtually stammering. I stopped trying to reach for the Coke that some sympathetic soul pushed my way because my hands were shaking too much. My colleagues listened to my idea . . . but it was a bad idea and I knew it.

This executive was given the "power" to do an important task, but clearly he lacked of a sense of competence for it. He felt out of his league, not ready to bare his ideas to the company. Though good managers stretch people so that they are constantly learning and growing, it is important to stretch them in ways that help build their sense of competence rather than causing them to fall flat on their faces. When people don't have a sense of confidence in their ability to do their work, they tend to become paralyzed and withdraw from the task at hand. The result often is high levels of absenteeism or turnover. Building a sense of competence can also be important for retaining the best talent. Michael Schlow, chef and co-owner of Radius, one of Boston's hippest restaurants, realized that money had little to do with keeping his best young cooks from jumping ship. They were most often leaving so they could learn more. So he decided to run his kitchen like a cooking school, where his people would continually update their capability and skills. One ongoing assignment is for each person to share the latest news and trends in the restaurant business. Each day, a member of the kitchen staff is responsible for researching information about food and presenting it at the daily staff meeting. There are even thirty-minute exams about the restaurant, its cuisine, and staff.[6] Schlow recognized that good people *want* to stretch their abilities, and he provided the means for them to do so.

Impact

Impact is the degree to which people can influence their surroundings and to which their work units and organizations listen to their ideas. Impact is people having input into strategic, administrative, and operating decisions. Empowered individuals believe that what they do has impact; in short, they see themselves as making a difference. They do not experience what psychologists call a sense of "learned helplessness"; they see themselves as active participants in shaping the direction and outcomes of the larger system in which they are embedded. Consequently, they believe they can challenge existing organizational mindsets and push organizational boundaries. It is through this lens of personal control that empowered individuals see the world and choose to act.

This aspect of empowerment relates directly to the need for current organizations to be quick on their feet and responsive to change. In our interviews, individuals who expressed a sense of personal control articulated a mindset of change rather than regulation or maintenance. They viewed change as a necessary and vital part of their role in the organization, and they felt that they had some control over such change. Here are some examples:

- "I don't assume that the current situation is a given. I think about how things can be different and better and develop a new vision on which I act. I know that I can make a difference."
- "I usually feel empowered in times of crisis and difficulty. I feel very challenged because the outcome of the situation is usually pretty uncertain, but I know that ultimately with a lot of hard work, I can have an impact."
- "Empowerment means doing things that have an effect on the company. It's making a difference through my work."
- "Our division was contemplating some major restructurings, and it was not at all clear where our department would fall in the move. There were rumors that we would be absorbed into other departments. Though our jobs were not immediately on the line, we knew that it would be a mistake for the division to disband our department for a number of reasons I won't go into here. I knew we had to take action with top management. [Some details deleted here.] In the end, we did save our department and actually had our responsibilities expanded."

The Interdependence of the Four Dimensions

An important lesson that emerges from this account of empowerment is that all four of the dimensions we have discussed are necessary for people to feel genuinely empowered; any one dimension is only part of the equation. In other words, the dimensions combine multiplicatively rather than additively. If any one dimension is missing, a person will not feel empowered, even if the other three dimensions exist.

For example, in one service organization, employees were asked to take part in a strategic decision-making process. These individuals felt a sense of meaning (they cared about the company and its future direction), a sense of self-determination (they were part of the decision-making process) and a sense of impact (they felt able to influence the process), but they felt overwhelmed by the request. They had never been involved in strategic decision making before and didn't feel that they had the capability to contribute effectively. In short, they felt little sense of competence. As a result, these "empowered" individuals were largely silent.

In another example, employees were delegated the decision about what color to repaint the walls of the production facility in a remodeling. Clearly, they experienced a sense of self-determination (it was their decision) and competence (they have the ability to make a good decision), but they lacked a sense of meaning (they really didn't care what color the walls were) and impact (the decision had little bearing about what they actually did in their jobs or on the organization's performance).

These examples illustrate a crucial reason that many empowerment efforts have failed: They focused on only one or two dimensions of empowerment—often just emphasizing the autonomy that comes with self-determination and neglecting the others. An organization that seeks to release the leadership capabilities of its employees must develop all four dimensions.

■ Outcomes of Empowerment

Self-determination, meaning, competence, and impact: If this is what genuine empowerment means, it is perhaps not hard to see why many employees would value feeling empowered. But how does the organization benefit by creating the conditions in which this kind of empowerment can happen? What can we expect from empowered people?

We have conducted research on hundreds of employees (from lower-level service workers to middle-level managers) in many different kinds of organizations (from high-technology firms to *Fortune* 500 manufacturing companies to health sector entities to government bureaucracies). Our research suggests that empowerment, as we have defined it, produces specific outcomes that can create a significant competitive advantage for today's organizations.

- Empowered individuals see themselves as more *effective* in their work and are evaluated as more effective by those with whom they work.[7]
- Empowered employees are *less resistant to change* in the context of major organizational change such as downsizing because they tend to be more hopeful that organization problems can be overcome.[8]
- Empowered individuals are more *innovative* and not afraid to try new things.[9]
- Empowered individuals are *transformational in their leadership ability.* They are more likely to engage in upward-influence activities with their boss.[10]
- Empowered individuals report *making transformational change* (as opposed to more incremental types of adjustments) when stimulated to make change.[11]
- Empowered leaders are seen as *charismatic* by their followers, a quality that enhances their ability to bring transformational change to their organization.[12]
- Empowered individuals are more satisfied with their work, and their sense of competence reduces job-related strain.[13]

In today's fast-paced, global economy, people who are more effective, innovative, open to change, and transformational in their leadership abilities are very attractive indeed. They are the kind of workers who make an organization stand out from its competitors. They are, in a word, *leaders.* And in today's business environment, a company of leaders can be an important source of competitive advantage.

■ What Organizations and Managers Can Do

Earlier, we indicated that one of the key reasons for the failure of past empowerment efforts was the misunderstanding of how genuine empowerment is achieved. No one can empower anyone else; empowerment comes from within the individual. What managers and organizations can do is create the conditions in which self-empowerment flourishes. This effort goes well beyond simply delegating responsibility or pronouncing that people are henceforward "empowered." It involves a personal change on the part of leadership and a culture change on the part of organizations. How you can go about making these changes is the focus of this book. We draw from findings from our research and practice to offer specific strategies, tools, and techniques that you can follow to develop a company of leaders. Real-life examples from organizations that have adopted these approaches are highlighted throughout.

In the chapters that follow, we introduce what we call the five disciplines for unleashing the power within people. In Chapter Two, we demonstrate that these disciplines are not quick and easy fixes but approaches that require hard work and persistence. In that chapter, we also make clear that genuine empowerment involves an inherent tension, a sort of paradox composed of seemingly opposite forces that must coexist: on one hand, freedom and personal liberation, which require trust and an openness to risk; on the other hand, direction, security, and support, which require more control and guidance.

In Chapter Three, we show how the first discipline sets the stage for the others. It emphasizes that in creating an empowering system, we must first empower ourselves. Only if we model an empowered mindset and behavior to others can we expect them to follow suit. To help benchmark your own empowerment, we offer a personal assessment.

In Chapters Four through Seven, we describe how to create a context that unleashes the power within your workforce. In Chapter Four, we introduce the second discipline, the need for a clear vision and challenge to "hook" people to the organization and its mission. We introduce the third discipline of security and support in Chapter Five, which is so critical for enabling employees to feel the psychological safety necessary for initiative and risk taking. In Chapter Six, we describe the fourth discipline of openness and trust, focusing on how to create a culture that truly values its human assets. Then in Chapter Seven, we discuss the need for guidance and control, the fifth and last discipline, so that employees know the boundaries of their empowerment. And finally, in Chapter Eight, we address some specific recommendations on how to apply the disciplines to your organization. We close the book with a discussion of whether there are certain types of employees who can't or perhaps shouldn't be empowered.

As an additional aid to help bring the ideas of this book alive and personalize them, we encourage you to begin an empowerment journal. Before proceeding any further, take a moment to locate a small notebook or pad of paper to record your journal entries. Keep it at your side as you work through the book. Wherever you see the icon 📖 sprinkled throughout the book, pause for a moment and complete a journal entry. Each should take no more than a couple of minutes but will help you make personal connections with the material, as well as create an agenda for action as you begin to create your own company of leaders. Before concluding this chapter, take a moment to create your first journal entry below.

 Reflect on your own experiences with empowerment by responding to the following questions.

- What does the word *empowerment* mean to you? How is it different from the definition we offer from our research?
- What has your experience been with empowerment in your workplace? If you had a negative experience, what reasons do you attribute to the failure of the empowerment initiative?
- What would you like to get out of this book to help you create your own company of leaders?

CHAPTER SUMMARY

Creating a company of leaders—a high-performance workplace in which employees willingly do their best work and act as owners of the business—is both a strategic advantage and a necessity for attracting and retaining the best people. Leadership, in this sense, is a direct outcome of creating conditions of empowerment. Unfortunately, the once-fashionable notion of empowerment has suffered from the failure of empowerment programs to achieve their intended results. The solution, however, is not to discard what was true and valuable about the idea of empowerment but to rescue the kernels of truth in this concept, learn from both research and experience, and build a new and more effective understanding of the conditions that foster genuine empowerment.

In this chapter we have taken key learnings from research and practice to burn away some of the debris weighing down the notion of empowerment and identify its central core. This core is a mindset characterized by self-determination, meaning, competence, and impact. All four of these dimensions are necessary to release the energy, creativity, and initiative in an organization's workforce. When people feel genuinely empowered, they exhibit the kind of leadership qualities that can be a strategic advantage to any organization.

But creating the conditions required for genuine empowerment is not easy. It involves significant changes in the behavior of executives and managers as well as a deep understanding of what empowerment is. In the next chapter, we draw on our research and practice to identify the five disciplines of empowerment. As you will see, each discipline is in creative tension with the others. Implementing these disciplines requires that managers and executives maintain a delicate balance among them while focusing relentlessly on shaping a workplace that nourishes leadership at all levels.

Five Disciplines for Unleashing the Power in Your Workforce

I n Chapter One we argued that an organization of leaders is a powerful source of competitive advantage. Therefore, we might expect all managers to strive to build a company of leaders. Wrong!

Strategists tell us that real competitive advantage is difficult to imitate. Why? Because creating a real competitive advantage requires more discipline than normal people are willing to exercise. Competitive advantage comes from doing some hard things that others were not willing to do.

Consider again the case of Southwest Airlines. Several years ago, the major airlines tried to imitate Southwest's amazing success as a low-cost, no-frills carrier. Continental Airlines and

United attempted to replicate Southwest's success by creating new no-frills airlines within an airline. Both copied Southwest's policies of eliminating meals and advance seating assignments. Like Southwest, they relied exclusively on 737 planes to minimize maintenance and training needs. They believed they would have little problem capturing the key elements of Southwest's success.

After many millions of dollars invested, both airlines failed. Continental's Lite airline folded, and United's Shuttle has not achieved cost or performance targets even close to those of Southwest. Why? Because they were not able to imitate the real source of Southwest Airlines' competitive advantage—its workforce. Southwest has created a system that energizes its people to be more productive and work more hours than any other airline. They have hundreds of people applying for each of their jobs and turnover rates that are by far the lowest in the industry. And they don't do it by offering higher levels of pay. Instead, they create a work environment that attracts good people and unleashes their power to contribute.

Creating real competitive advantage is never easy. That is one of the lessons of failed empowerment efforts. Empowerment is not just another program to be implemented by the human resources or quality departments. It cannot be achieved by crossing off items on a checklist. It does not happen by telling people that they are empowered. It comes from creating a culture in which people develop a mindset characterized by a sense of self-determination, meaning, competence, and impact. And that does not happen overnight.

Experience shows that managers and executives often find it difficult to complete the journey to genuine empowerment. Some don't have the courage to begin. Some get lost along the way. Some stumble and decide to turn around when they are only part of the way there. Many confuse empowerment with a quick fix and give up on it before it has really been tried.

Part of the problem is an insufficient understanding of what genuine empowerment requires of leaders, managers, and organizations. The aim of this chapter is to continue our controlled burn on empowerment notions by introducing what we call the five disciplines of empowerment. These are the disciplines that our research shows are essential to creating a company of leaders. They are not magic bullets; they take dedication, hard work, and persistence. To better understand what implementing these disciplines involves, let's begin by exploring the parallels between undertaking a true empowerment effort and the preparations a novice runner makes for competing in a marathon.

■ Like Training for a Marathon: Commitment, Consistency, and Investment

 Have you ever subjected your body and spirit to a grueling physical challenge such as climbing a mountain or running a marathon—one in which you aren't sure you can actually complete the challenge, in which you feel fully extended? In your empowerment journal, note how this experience made you feel. How did you ward off exhaustion to maintain your momentum?

This kind of intense experience has many parallels to the empowerment process. Like preparing for a marathon, the journey to empowerment requires sustained discipline, hard work, courage, and mental stamina.

Personal Commitment

Several years ago, a good friend who was a novice runner decided that she wanted to run in a marathon. The problem was that there were unending distractions, including a new project at work and a child to take care of. One particularly cold winter morning Pam woke and made a decision. She would begin that very day to train. If she kept letting the other commitments in her life interfere with her goal, she would never realize her dream.

What was most important is that Pam herself made the decision. Imagine if her husband or her boss told her she *had* to run a marathon. She probably would have found a variety of "good" excuses for why this wasn't the right time and would have blamed her husband or her boss when she suffered her first bout of blisters, aches, and pains. When the first opportunity came along to bow out of the marathon, she probably would have seized it.

The same is true of empowerment. Real empowerment is something that individuals must *choose* to have because they want to be empowered. Recall that one part of an empowered mindset is self-determination. This choice element is critical for building an empowered workforce. Empowerment cannot be mandated, and it cannot be forced. Telling someone to be empowered is like telling someone to be spontaneous. People must want to be empowered, and they must make a personal commitment for it to happen.

Similarly, as we will demonstrate, managers must make a personal commitment to modify their behavior in a way that promotes this kind of mindset. That is one of the crucial messages of this book: To create a climate of empowerment, we must first change ourselves. We cannot have an empowered organization if we behave as we have always behaved. We have to make the commitment to clarify our own values and be willing to act in ways that are consistent with expecting leadership from others.

Part of this commitment is choosing to see the process through, to commit to the long haul. When Pam made her decision to run in the marathon, it was not something that she could go out and do the next day. When she began her training, she could barely run a mile. She had to start with short runs interspersed with walking and had to build up to long-distance running. Had she treated her commitment like most of us treat our New Year's resolutions, she would have tried it for a week, burned out, and gone back to life as usual.

Like training for a marathon, building a climate of empowerment takes time and a sustained, disciplined approach. For example, at Delphi's Oak Creek assembly plant in Michigan, workers were frightened, angry, and resistant to changes aimed at creating more employee involvement.[1] Employees were being asked to work as part of quality circles. The company's managers knew that the company could not survive without the commitment of the workforce. For six months there was little progress; workers simply did not believe that the company was committed to the change. Yet management persisted in the face of the discouraging resistance. This behavior eventually became a signal that management's commitment to employee involvement was real. Slowly, workers began to respond by taking initiative, offering suggestions, and making improvements. With small successes, trust began to grow. Gradually a flood of ideas and initiatives came forth.

Today, those same people work in self-managing teams or "cells" where they determine their own schedules, inspect products for quality and productivity, and communicate directly with customers. The empowerment effort is considered a dramatic success. Costs are down and productivity is way up. But most important, employees act as leaders.

In most companies, that success would never have been achieved. Too often the concept of empowerment sounds nice until people realize that they must commit time and energy to a difficult and long-term process of behavioral change. Without an adequate understanding of the kind of commitment involved, they are like people who give up on the idea of competing in a marathon when their first efforts leave them breathless and aching after they have run only a mile.

In your empowerment journal, describe your level of commitment to empowerment in your workplace. What kind of expectations do you have? What is your time table? Are you committed for the long haul?

Consistency, Consistency, Consistency

Having made her personal commitment, Pam needed to develop a consistent training schedule. To avoid injury, she needed a routine that included beginning and ending her runs with stretching exercises. She had to maintain consistent discipline. She couldn't save her training for the weekends when she had more free time. She had to say no to distracting activities. When her boss needed her to travel, she took along her running gear and declined early morning meetings so she could maintain her schedule. She entered her training time on her Palm Pilot just as she did any other meeting. She negotiated with her husband to take care of some of her home responsibilities.

This kind of consistency is also necessary when we set out to change cultures and behaviors. We have to focus our energies and carve out time for creating a system that fosters empowerment. There will always be pressures to preserve the status quo: to stick with tried-and-true behaviors and avoid taking on new challenges. Resisting those pressures is a key to making the process of empowerment work. If managers are wishy-washy, if their efforts are not focused, their initiative will lack impact. They need to forego activities and behaviors that are contrary to creating a mindset of empowerment. They need to take care not to send mixed messages about what is desired and proclaim a clear message that leadership behavior is a priority. And they need to make sure that their actions are consistent with their rhetoric.

Is there consistency between what you say and what you do regarding empowerment? Document at least one example of when your behaviors did not support empowerment. What could you do differently?

Making the Investment

As Pam soon discovered, preparing to run in a marathon requires making investments: a good pair of running shoes, the right support garments, and nonbinding clothing. It would have been easy for her to say that she could save money by getting by with what she had. But the wrong equipment, such as shoes that were worn out or designed for tennis as opposed to running, could have impaired her training and even caused injury.

Empowerment, too, requires investments. We may need to invest money in training and new technology to equip people to take needed initiatives. We may need to invest in a significant cultural change effort. It is futile to speak of being committed to the empowerment process without also being willing to invest in the resources that make genuine empowerment possible.

 What investments have you made toward empowerment? Think about how you may be short-changing empowerment. What potential problems could this kind of short-changing create?

■ A Preview of the Disciplines

Our analogy of the marathon runner has emphasized the need for personal commitment, consistency, and the willingness to make appropriate investments. But even the strongest-willed marathon runner needs something more: she needs to know *how* to train, how to pace herself, even how to breathe. In a similar way, many empowerment efforts have failed for lack of specific know-how, a clear-eyed understanding of exactly what to *do* to create and foster a climate of leadership.

That is what our five disciplines of empowerment aim to provide. We choose the word *disciplines* very deliberately to suggest the kind of self-control, regular attention, practice, sacrifice, and practical know-how that genuine empowerment requires.

Together the five disciplines stimulate the creative tension that is needed to maintain a climate that fosters leadership at all levels of the organization.

Here we provide an overview of the five disciplines and consider the underlying tensions among them—something that often has not been appreciated in empowerment efforts. The chapters that follow lay out the logic of each of these disciplines and provide specific examples, tools, techniques, and strategies for implementing them.

The First Discipline: Empowering Yourself

The first discipline—*empowering yourself*—sets the stage for the others. If we want others to act like leaders, we must first model the kind of behavior that we expect. To do so, we need to ensure that we ourselves have a sense of self-determination, meaning, competence, and impact in our own work. If we do not, how can we ask our employees to have this mindset?

Our first step, then, must be to assess the level of our own empowerment. This means asking, Who am I? What do I want to be? What is my current level of personal empowerment? Empowerment isn't about preaching, and it isn't about learning ways to get others to be something that we ourselves are not. The empowered leader is a role model who knows that actions speak louder than words.

The Second Discipline: Continuous Vision and Challenge

The second discipline consists of creating *a clear vision and challenge* to "hook" people to the organization and its mission. As Dennis Bakke, CEO of AES, the global electricity company, has articulated,

Our main goal at the beginning was to build a company that we ourselves would want to work in. The actual type of business wasn't really important, to tell you the truth. It could have been an energy conservation company; it could have been steel. The struggle before the deal, for instance, the challenge and creativity required to make it work, taking risks, and even sleepless nights—believe it or not, those things are really fun because they engage people—heart, mind, and soul. And that was the kind of company we set out to create, one in which people could have engaging experiences on a daily basis.[2]

Our research confirms the wisdom of Bakke's observations. Highly empowered people feel that they understand top management's vision and the strategic direction of the organization. This understanding depends on employees' having access to strategic information about the organization's future direction. Only if they have such information can they take initiative or introduce innovations to advance the organization's goals. Together with a shared vision, this kind of knowledge provides a clear direction so that employees feel they can act autonomously rather than waiting for permission and direction from those in authority. Further, to enlist everyone's best efforts, the vision must provide challenge to employees, thus stretching their capability to improve themselves and the organization.

The Third Discipline: Continuous Security and Support

The third discipline consists of providing adequate *security and support*. For employees to feel that the system really wants them to act like leaders, they need a sense of social support from their bosses, peers, and subordinates. Accordingly, their efforts to take initiative and risk must be reinforced rather than punished. They must believe that the company will support them as they learn and grow. If this support is weak or missing—if, for example, risk taking is punished when it doesn't turn out well, or if successes are not praised and publicized—employees will worry about seeking permission before acting rather than asking for forgiveness if they make mistakes. This point is exemplified in an often-told story at UPS. Some years ago, an employee went beyond the bounds of his authority to order an extra 737 to ensure timely delivery of a trainload of packages left behind in the Christmas rush. Rather than punish the employee, UPS praised his initiative, and the story survives as proof that the company stands behind such empowered action.

The Fourth Discipline: Continuous Openness and Trust

The fourth discipline involves creating a climate of *openness and trust.* Part of feeling empowered is knowing that the corporate culture emphasizes the value of the human assets in the organization. As difficult as it is to build such a culture in an environment of downsizing and rapid change, it is essential for employees to feel a sense of participation, openness, concern, and trust. Empowered employees feel that the people in their unit work together to solve problems and that employees' ideas are taken seriously in decision making.

Creating an environment that trusts people to think for themselves and take chances means loosening controls rather than tightening them. It means organizing not more, but less. Roger Sant, the chairman of AES, expresses the point well: "Never tell people how to do their jobs. Instead, present them with a challenge, and then let them choose the best way to attack it. Even when I have an idea or plan, I try to invite people to be part of the problem solving. That way they feel part of the team—and they usually come up with an idea that is better than mine."[3]

The Fifth Discipline: Continuous Guidance and Control

The fifth and final discipline involves providing adequate *guidance and control*. Genuine empowerment doesn't mean that people are turned loose to do whatever they want. In fact, highly empowered people report that they work in units with clear goals, clear lines of authority, and clear task responsibilities. Though they have autonomy, they are aware of the boundaries of their decision-making discretion. They know what they are responsible for achieving and what others have responsibility for. They have clear goals and objectives that are aligned with the vision of the organization.

The key focus of this lever is to reduce the disabling uncertainty and ambiguity that so often accompany empowerment efforts. For example, Marriott has developed "safe zones" so that employees understand which kind of situations allow for empowerment and which do not. These safe zones set boundaries for empowered behavior; they let people know how far they can go with their empowerment. Calling in maintenance to fix a light without approval may be OK, but purchasing a new light may be beyond their safe zone. Without a basic level of structure and control, employees experience chaos rather than empowerment.

■ **Underlying Tensions in the Disciplines of Empowerment**

You may have already noticed a key point about the five disciplines that we have described: Some seem almost in conflict with others. On one hand, empowerment involves a sense of personal autonomy that requires trust and an openness to risk. On the other hand, empowerment requires security, support, control, and guidance. You might well ask, Well, then, which is it? Autonomy or direction? Self-confidence or security and support?

Balancing Opposing Forces

Our answer is all of the above. Our research has revealed that genuine empowerment involves implicit tensions. The challenge for managers is not to choose one aspect of empowerment over another, but rather to balance a set of opposing forces that must coexist.

These creative tensions are illustrated in Figure 2.1. The first discipline, *empowering yourself,* which undergirds all the others, contrasts with the other disciplines in that it is focused on the self whereas the other four are focused on the system and context. So the first tension of empowerment involves the need to focus simultaneously on the self and the system. Managers who focus on the self without recognizing and working to change the system they are part of will be too inner-oriented and are likely to be ineffectual in eliciting leadership behaviors from others. By the same token, managers who focus on the system but not the self are likely to behave hypocritically, expecting things of others that they do not model themselves.

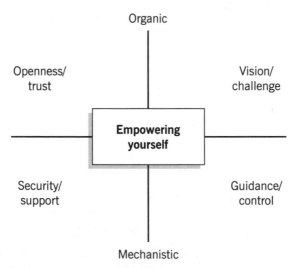

Figure 2.1. The Creative Tensions of the Disciplines of Empowerment

The second tension involves the inherent contrast between the disciplines of openness/trust and guidance/control. On one hand, the system must liberate and give power to individuals to act as they see appropriate. On the other hand, the system must maintain control, providing guidance when necessary and setting boundaries. Focusing on freedom without setting appropriate boundaries is likely to produce the "loose cannons" that many organizations fear. But focusing too much on boundaries and guidance will discourage the initiative that empowerment is meant to foster. Both disciplines need to coexist in creative harmony to make empowerment work.

The third tension is between the disciplines of vision/challenge and security/support. On one hand, the system must be future looking, focused on stretching people in new ways to reach their full potential. On the other hand, the system must provide a sense of security and support so that people develop confidence and competence. If we stretch people too much without requisite support systems, they will feel overwhelmed. If we emphasize security without sufficient stretch, the system will become stagnant and people will not be prepared to respond dynamically to changes in the larger environment.

These observations bring us to the last of the mistaken ideas about empowerment that we need to burn away: that empowerment must come at the expense of values such as control and security, or that adequate control can only be maintained if people do not exercise real power and autonomy. Rather, genuine empowerment requires a willingness to deal with its inherent tensions and maintain a delicate balance of the five disciplines. A company of leaders is not anarchy—but neither is it the traditional command-and-control structure in which only those in authority act with autonomy and initiative. Empowerment, then, involves an apparent paradox—but it is precisely this paradoxical quality that we find in truly empowered organizations.

How do you experience the competing tensions of empowerment? Write down two examples of when you felt the paradoxical quality of empowerment.

Organic versus Mechanistic Perspectives on Empowerment

To further appreciate the inherent tensions of empowerment, consider the following scenario.

A number of years ago, we had the opportunity to work with a *Fortune* 500 manufacturing company that was struggling to maintain its competitive edge in the marketplace. The members of the top management team could see that the organization was on a downward trajectory and that some kind of initiative was required to get it back on track. Their proposed solution was to empower their workforce, and they proceeded to make empowerment a top priority in their business plan. After a frustrating year with little apparent progress, they asked us to diagnose why empowerment wasn't working.

We began by individually interviewing the twelve most senior people in the organization. We asked them to define empowerment and to describe what is necessary to facilitate it. The interviews were revealing, because they uncovered sharp differences in the senior managers' views about how one "empowers" people.

Half of the senior managers believed that empowerment was about delegation and accountability. To them, empowerment was a top-down process whereby senior management developed a clear vision and then communicated specific plans and assignments to the rest of the organization. Top management would provide employees with the information and resources needed to help them accomplish their tasks. Then employees would make the required procedural changes and process improvements. The result was greater managerial control, increased clarification, and simplification of employees' work.

In short, this group of senior managers believed that empowerment was about delegating decision making within a set of clear boundaries and scope. Their implicit strategy for empowerment was

- Start at the top
- Clarify the organization's mission, vision, and values
- Clearly specify the tasks, roles, and rewards for employees
- Delegate responsibility
- Hold people accountable for results

The second half of the senior managers saw empowerment quite differently. They believed that empowerment was about risk taking, growth, and change. Empowerment meant trusting people and tolerating their imperfections. When it came to rules, the senior managers in this group believed that the existing structures often presented a barrier to doing the right thing for the company. They assumed that newly empowered employees would naturally make some mistakes but that they should not be punished. Empowered employees would be entrepreneurs and risk takers with a sense of ownership and commitment for the organization. They would engage in creative conflict by constantly challenging each other. Exposing and resolving differences would create a synergy among empowered employees.

In short, this group of senior managers saw empowerment as a process of risk taking and personal growth. Their implicit strategy for empowerment was

- Start at the bottom by understanding the needs of the employee
- Model empowered behavior for the employees
- Build teams to encourage cooperative behavior
- Encourage intelligent risk taking
- Trust people to perform

These two perspectives on empowerment seem irreconcilable. We call the first group's perspective, with its top-down view, a *mechanistic* approach to empowerment. In contrast, we call the second group's perspective, with its bottom-up view, an *organic* approach. The most important contrast between these two perspectives involves the implicit assumptions people make about trust and control.

When we relayed our observations to the senior management team, they were uncharacteristically silent. Finally, someone from the first perspective expressed a core concern about the second group's viewpoint on empowerment: "We cannot afford loose cannons around here." A person from the second group retorted, "When was the last time you saw a cannon of any kind around here?" An intense argument followed. Neither group could understand the other's perspective. Not surprisingly, the top management team eventually dropped the notion of empowerment from their business plans.[4]

The surfacing of the contrasting set of assumptions made it clear to us why the senior managers had made little headway in their objective to empower the workforce. Though all the executives seemed in agreement that the empowerment of the workforce was the right thing to do, they were in deep conflict over the meaning of empowerment and how it should be implemented in their organization. Such conflicts or tensions are common in contemporary organizations and represent a primary reason that empowerment efforts are likely to fail.

After hearing this story, the first question many people ask is, Which perspective is right? Before answering this question, let's take a closer look at each of the two perspectives.

The mechanistic perspective begins with a mandate from senior management, often in response to a strong need to cut costs or increase productivity. It is typically reactive and implemented when there are few resources available. In recent years, it has often been implemented in conjunction with downsizing.

In this approach, senior management develops a vision of where the organization needs to go and then solicits buy-in to the vision from the rest of the organization. Specific plans and assignments are cascaded throughout the organization so people know exactly what needs to be done. Roles are clearly defined. Information is shared more than before, but only to the extent that it is needed for people to perform their immediate jobs. Limited resources are made available for specific, well-defined needs, but often people are asked to "do more with less."

Decision making is delegated to lower-level employees but is limited to decisions that directly relate to one's own job, often with strict guidelines about what is allowed and what still needs approval. Decision-making rules and performance management processes ensure accountability. When people know precisely what needs to be done, they don't need as much direct supervision, especially when they are held directly accountable for their results.

Our experience is that most people are more comfortable with the mechanistic perspective on empowerment. This viewpoint tends to be consistent with more conventional management practices. As such, it tends to receive the lion's share of attention in the popular business press. Both senior management and much of the workforce feels comfortable with this perspective because the whole process is controlled with a clear sense for where the organization is going and what needs to be done. Employees are asked to do more but with greater accountability and more information, yet also within well-specified boundaries. The vision gets implemented, but with little creativity or exploration. Employees feel more ownership than in a traditional hierarchical system, but the improvement is incremental.

If the core of the mechanistic approach is control, the core of the organic approach is freedom or liberation. Rather than the top-down approach characteristic of the mechanistic perspective, the organic perspective tends to begin at the lower levels of the organization. Managers put a priority on understanding the dreams and aspirations of all employees. What energizes them? What turns them on? The assumption is that if we want people to act as owners of the firm, they must have a strong personal connection to the organization—it must be part of their identity as humans. They must believe in the mission of the organization in a very personal way. An example of this ideal is the janitor at NASA who sees her job not as taking out the trash, but as helping to put an astronaut onto the moon.

In contrast to the clear roles and responsibilities of the mechanistic system, the organic system is more open and free-form. *Trust* becomes the operative term. Employees are trusted to do the right thing. This means tolerating imperfections and recognizing that people will make mistakes. It means encouraging an attitude of asking for forgiveness if mistakes are made rather than asking for permission to act at all.

Managers may feel uncomfortable with this approach when people do things their own way, not just the way that a manager thinks is best. But this discomfort is recognized as the price of encouraging people to feel a sense of ownership. At the same time, there is a recognition that employees need a clear sense of vision and of what ends to aim for, even when the means to those ends are unspecified. It is assumed that people will need training and developing so they have the appropriate expertise to make the kind of decisions that often have been the domain of higher-level managers.

The results of this perspective are often real breakthrough ideas and creativity as people bring their full potential to the organization. At the same time, there are likely to be feelings of uncertainty and ambiguity as people struggle to figure out how to coordinate their autonomous activities with others. There is also the very real potential for "loose cannons," employees who are out to serve their own interests at the expense of the organization.

 Which of the two perspectives do you tend to resonate with? Why?

Blending the Best of Both Perspectives

Although it will be obvious that the organic perspective captures much of what we have claimed for genuine empowerment, our discussion of the creative tensions in empowerment suggests that, in fact, neither perspective is "right" by itself. Each brings some important strengths but also some important limitations.

As with the disciplines of empowerment, our contention is that both perspectives are correct—but only when combined with each other. Otherwise, either perspective can degenerate into its extreme. The mechanistic approach to empowerment can degenerate into a traditional bureaucratic system with excessive controls. The organic system can degenerate into a system plagued with chaotic self-expression that has little alignment with the collective vision. Genuine empowerment requires a *both-and* perspective rather than an *either-or* solution. Instead of a choice between the mechanistic and organic views, it requires the integration of the truth in both.

To most people, this need for creative tension is uncomfortable and unsettling. Often in organizational life, we exert energy to *reduce* ambiguity, not to *foster* it. But sustained empowerment requires both perspectives together, and this is what makes the challenge of forging a company of leaders so cognitively and behaviorally complex. In the remaining chapters, we try to show how the challenge can be met.

CHAPTER SUMMARY

Creating a company of leaders does not come cheaply or easily. It requires the kind of sustained effort exemplified by a runner training for a marathon: commitment, consistency, and a willingness to make necessary investments.

Genuine empowerment also requires knowing what to do. The five disciplines of empowerment capture the conditions that we have observed to be essential in creating a climate that fosters leadership at all levels. The word *disciplines* is key: To engage in disciplines is to be committed to a dedicated effort of genuine behavioral and systemic change.

The five disciplines also express an aspect of empowerment that is too little understood—namely, that true empowerment involves a creative tension between opposing forces. Vision and challenge must be balanced with support and security, openness and trust with guidance and control. At the most fundamental level, self-empowerment must be balanced with attention to the system in which we operate.

Too often empowerment efforts flounder between competing visions of what empowerment means: whether it is a top-down process of delegation, or a bottom-up process of liberation. In our view, empowerment is both—together.

This more complete understanding of empowerment prepares the way for the detailed discussion of the five disciplines in subsequent chapters. No strategies or techniques can take the place of authentic commitment to the ideal of encouraging leadership throughout the organization. Nor can any quick fix eliminate the inherent tensions in empowerment. But once the commitment is made and the need for holding the disciplines of empowerment in creative tension is accepted, the next question becomes how to go about creating that climate of leadership in which people feel genuinely empowered. We turn to that question now.

The First Discipline

Empower the Person
Who Matters Most

This discipline focuses on you. Before you can think about empowering others, you have to first look into the mirror, because "as a leader, the most important relationship you can cultivate is your relationship with yourself."[1] In the book *Deep Change,* Bob Quinn shares a story about a management team that had invested heavily in changing the culture of its company. All the senior people had attended a seminar on quality and had returned with enthusiasm for implementing the ideas they had learned within their organization. They shared with Bob how they expected that "quality, morale, productivity, and profit" would all improve because of the new philosophy and the clear expectations that had been set for everyone in the company. As Bob relates, what happened next was revealing:

Upon hearing their comments, I shared with them a story that was told to me by a vice president at another company. Three years before, that company had sent all its senior team to the same seminar. They also anticipated that their new plan would launch dramatic improvements in quality, morale, productivity, and profit. However, three years later, they found that their immense effort had little, if any, impact.

Given the sizable investment they had already made, the management team was transfixed by my story. They waited anxiously for an explanation of the failure. Almost in unison they asked, "Why did it fail?" Instead of providing an explanation I asked them to tell me why it failed.

A long, heavy silence permeated the room. Finally, one of the most influential members of the group said, "The leadership of the company didn't change their behavior." I nodded and pointed out that they themselves had made a lot of assumptions about the behavior that was going to change in others. Now I challenged them, "Identify one time when one of you said that you were going to change your behavior."

Again there was a long pause. Something important and unusual was happening. This group was suddenly seeing something that few people ever clearly see—the incongruity of asking for change in others while failing to exhibit the same level of commitment in self.

Since they expressed a sincere desire to change their organization, they asked me for advice. I described some simple practices that had worked successfully for others. These practices would give them the tools they needed to change their stagnant patterns and systems. They were quiet for a time; a time of quiet terror and inner reflection. It was as if they were standing at the edge of a very dangerous cliff and peeking over. They decided to adjourn and think about the issues.[2]

Here is a dismaying tale of managers whose enthusiasm for deep change seems to evaporate the moment they begin to realize that the change must start with themselves. Yet any of us could be the managers in this story. In confronting life's problems, all of us readily see how the shortcomings of others—the boss, a peer, a subordinate, a spouse, a child—contribute to the problem at hand. It is not natural for us to see our own role in preserving problematic patterns. Because the problem is "out there," it is always someone else who needs to change. When the issue involves our role as managers, we tend to use our authority to do the natural thing and tell *others* they must change their ways. When they do not, we look for ways to gain "leverage"— a polite way of saying we try to force them to change. Forcing changes in behavior may be successful in the short run, but in the long run it damages our relationships and undermines people's commitment.

The managers in Bob's story were trying to make a cultural change. Creating an empowering organization is also an effort in cultural change. As we suggested in Chapter One, the natural temptation for leaders is to simply tell people they are empowered and then return to their desks. When nothing much seems to happen, they get frustrated and look for someone, or something, to blame. But the problem is not with the workforce or with the concept of empowerment; the problem is that the leader has not understood the first discipline of empowerment.

This first discipline is *self-empowerment*. No one can tell anyone else to be free and self-determined, to find meaning in work, feel competent, or believe they have impact. The four dimensions of empowerment represent goals that each of us can achieve only for ourselves. But when we do empower ourselves, something happens. In examining the self-change represented in a process he called the hero's journey, Joseph Campbell noted that the hero always returns empowered and empowering to the community.[3] What this means is that when we exercise the courage to face our own fears, we are transformed. We start to see the world differently. We act differently. And our transformation changes the environment in a way that encourages other members of the community to empower themselves.

Consider the case of Paul, a senior executive in a large corporation that had undergone three downsizings in a short period.[4]

Paul graphically described his fears of losing his job and not being able to maintain his standard of living, send his children to college, or keep his home. After months of agony, Paul began to confront his fears and clarify his values. In doing so, he concluded that he had an identity separate from the organization and that he could survive on a much smaller salary if necessary. This change in perspective had an empowering effect. Paul stopped worrying about the dangers of change and how he was seen by the organization. He began to ask himself what was needed in the present. Paul saw his immobilized colleagues and realized that he needed to do something to empower them. He designed a new role for himself: Paul carefully selected people and invited them into meetings and asked them what they wanted the division to look like in ten years. Initially, they were startled by his question, but gradually, they joined in the process of designing the company's future. Paul's empowerment spread to others and things began to change.

Paul's story illustrates what we have found in our research: Empowered people are empowering people. They create an empowering context through their own behavior. In contrast, people who are insecure and unempowered cannot create environments where others are willing to risk empowering themselves.

There is a strong analogy here to an old adage in therapy about love: "Before we can love others, we must first love ourselves." In a similar way, if we are not ourselves empowered—if we don't have a strong sense of personal meaning, competence, self-determination, and impact—we will not feel comfortable giving up the kind of control that is necessary for real empowerment to occur. We will not be willing to make ourselves vulnerable to the actions and initiatives of others.

The discipline of self-empowerment focuses on the need to change ourselves so that our own mindset and behaviors are consistent with what we expect from others. Before asking others to behave as leaders, we must first be capable of empowered leadership. Only then will we be role models whose actions speak louder than words.

In thinking about self-empowerment, let us return to the word *discipline*. As we saw in the example of the marathon runner in the previous chapter, dedication to a discipline comes from the inside out. It requires strong personal commitment. If you are willing to undertake this discipline, the place to begin is with an assessment of your current level of empowerment. The next section provides a tested tool for performing this assessment and interpreting the results.

■ How Empowered Are You?

"Know thyself" is an ancient bit of wisdom, as old as the oracle at Delphi. But knowing oneself is the most difficult task any of us faces. It requires deep introspection. It means being willing to see ourselves without bias and defensiveness, warts and all. It means getting out of our comfort zone and being open to deep change.

In the case of empowerment, gaining a better understanding of yourself means asking questions such as these: How much meaning do you experience in your work? What level of confidence do you have about your capacity to do your work well—beyond expectations? How much freedom do you have to break from external constraints to do the right thing? How much impact do you have to really make a difference in your work environment? To help you probe these questions and assess your own level of empowerment, we provide the Psychological Empowerment Instrument (PEI) in Worksheet 3.1. This instrument has been validated through years of research on hundreds of people in many different industries, from diverse cultures, and at various levels of the organizational hierarchy. It has been found to be reliable across time and is a good predictor of the kind of empowered behaviors we find from employees who act as leaders.

The instrument is in the form of twelve questions focused on the four dimensions of psychological empowerment. After completing the instrument, you will be given instructions for how to score the assessment and create a profile of individual empowerment. Please take a few minutes right now to complete the assessment. Find a quiet spot where you can be reflective. Have the courage to be brutally honest with yourself. Only you will see your results, so use this as an opportunity to do some real self-examination.

Directions for Scoring the PEI

Scoring the Psychological Empowerment Instrument requires only simple arithmetic. Use the worksheet provided in Figure 3.1.

Once you have completed the scoring in Figure 3.1, the most effective way to interpret your scores is to plot or graph them. This helps you to see relationships, do comparisons, and identify patterns. Consequently, we encourage you to construct a picture of your psychological empowerment data by using the graph shown in Figure 3.2. Follow these steps:

■ Worksheet 3.1. The Psychological Empowerment Instrument ■

Using the following scale, please indicate the extent to which you agree or disagree that each statement describes how you see yourself in relation to your workplace.

1. Very strongly disagree		5. Agree
2. Strongly disagree	4. Neutral	6. Strongly agree
3. Disagree		7. Very strongly agree

____ a. I am confident about my ability to do my job.

____ b. The work that I do is important to me.

____ c. I have significant autonomy in determining how I do my job.

____ d. My impact on what happens in my department is large.

____ e. My job activities are personally meaningful to me.

____ f. I have a great deal of control over what happens in my department.

____ g. I can decide on my own how to go about doing my own work.

____ h. I have considerable opportunity for independence and freedom in how I do my job.

____ i. I have mastered the skills necessary for my job.

____ j. The work I do is meaningful to me.

____ k. I have significant influence over what happens in my department.

____ l. I am self-assured about my capabilities to perform my work activities.

Fill in your responses for each item in the PEI in the order shown below (items are identified by letter) and compute the indicated sums and averages.

Meaning	**(Example)**	**Competence**

b. ☐ +   4   a. ☐ +

e. ☐   3   i. ☐

j. ☐ +   4   l. ☐ +

─────────

☐ Sum (total of responses)   11   ☐ Sum (total of responses)

☐ Average (Sum divided by 3)   3.67   ☐ Average (Sum divided by 3)

Self-Determination   **Impact**

c. ☐ +   d. ☐ +

g. ☐   f. ☐

h. ☐ +   k. ☐ +

─────────

☐ Sum (total of responses)   ☐ Sum (total of responses)

☐ Average (Sum divided by 3)   ☐ Average (Sum divided by 3)

To calculate an overall empowerment score, calculate the mean (average) of the averages on the four dimensions:

☐ **Sum of empowerment** = Average of Meaning + Average of Competence + Average of Self-Determination + Average of Impact

☐ **Average of Empowerment Overall** = Sum of Empowerment divided by 4

Figure 3.1. Scoring the PEI

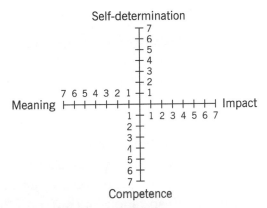

Figure 3.2. Your Individual Empowerment Profile

- Plot the average score you recorded for *meaning* on the left-hand line in Figure 3.2.
- Plot the average score for *self-determination* on the top line.
- Plot the average score for *competence* on the bottom line.
- Plot the average score for *impact* on the right-hand line.
- Finally, connect the points in each quadrant to form a four-sided figure. You will have produced a kite-like shape. This picture allows you to see readily the more and less dominant aspects of your empowerment profile.

It is important to remember that your empowerment profile is a snapshot at a point in time, not a personality description that tends to stay the same over the course of life. So you will want to update your profile as your job situation changes. For example, if you change jobs or companies, your empowerment profile is likely to look quite different. In the next section, we'll highlight some dominant profiles that yours may resemble. Afterwards, we'll provide some benchmarks for you to compare your dimension scores and overall empowerment scores against those of others.

Some Dominant Personal Profiles

The following set of profiles reflects the theoretical range of empowerment profiles. They reflect the possible extremes. It is likely that your own profile will resemble one of these dominant profiles. An understanding of what each profile might mean may be helpful to you in diagnosing and responding to trouble spots in your own empowerment profile.

The empowered leader profile is illustrated in Figure 3.3. Obviously, this person has high scores on all four dimensions. This profile is our ultimate aspiration for readers of this book. It indicates a person who can integrate the inherent tensions of empowerment.

The reality is that the majority of us are likely to start out with a strong quadrant or two, and a weak quadrant or two. Here are some profiles that are more likely to reflect our own profile. Suggestions for how to build up specific dimensions are provided later in this chapter.

The dreamer profile is illustrated in Figure 3.4. People with this profile score higher on the meaning dimension than on the others. Although they have a strong personal connection to their work, they fail to act on it because they do not feel that they have

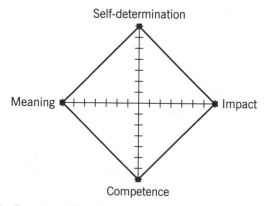

Figure 3.3. The Empowered Person

confidence or the autonomy to take initiative and have real impact. If this is you, your potential is not being realized. You have a strong sense of purpose or mission; now the challenge becomes how to act on it. Often the trigger for expanding this profile is to increase your confidence in your abilities so that you can then feel comfortable acting on your purpose.

The play-it-safe profile is illustrated in Figure 3.5. People with this profile have a strong sense of competence, yet they don't leverage this confidence in their abilities to show real initiative and have genuine impact. If this profile looks like yours, you are

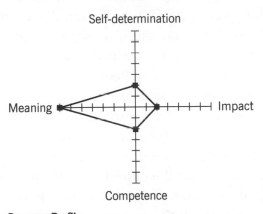

Figure 3.4. The Dreamer Profile

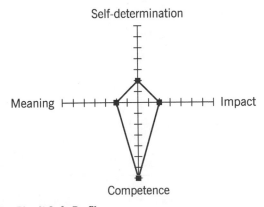

Figure 3.5. The Play-It-Safe Profile

not capitalizing on your capabilities to make a difference in your organization. The trigger for bettering this profile is to work hard to find meaning or purpose in your work. Often, when people have the competence but just don't care about their work, they are unlikely to want to take initiative in any significant way.

The do-it-my-way profile is illustrated in Figure 3.6. People with this profile have a high score on the self-determination dimension in comparison with the other dimensions. Though they act autonomously, they lack the sense of meaning and competence to make the most of their autonomy. If this is your profile, you are likely to be perceived as a loose cannon in the system—taking risks and feeling liberated even though you don't have the skills to make the most of your freedom of action. This is the profile that many companies are afraid will result from empowerment initiatives: People will act autonomously without the appropriate competencies or the mission to guide them. Once again, the trigger for bettering this profile is to build your capability so your initiatives have impact.

The tag-along profile is illustrated in Figure 3.7. People with this profile score high on the impact dimension in comparison with the other dimensions. They feel that they have impact even though they don't take initiative, have the requisite skills, or feel

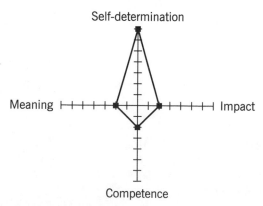

Figure 3.6. The Do-It-My-Way Profile

a meaningful connection to their organization. If this profile is similar to yours, then it is likely that you are having your impact through your reliance on others. You are having impact because you are in the right place at the right time, perhaps under the guidance of a strong leader. But because you are not taking initiative yourself and don't feel you have the right skills to perform well, you are dependent on others to make a difference.

The flexibility profile is illustrated in Figure 3.8. These people score high on meaning and self-determination in comparison to competence and impact. They tend to be adaptable as guided by their purpose, but because they don't have a strong sense of

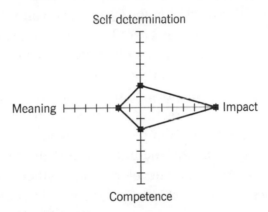

Figure 3.7. The Tag-Along Profile

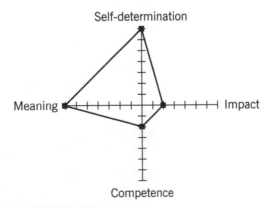

Figure 3.8. The Flexibility Profile

competence, they are unable to have significant impact. If this profile resembles yours, you are likely to find that building up your competence dimension will go a long way to developing the impact that is necessary to making you an empowered leader.

The stability profile is illustrated in Figure 3.9. This is the mirror image of the flexibility profile. These people score high on competence and impact in comparison to meaning and self-determination. The upshot is that they prefer control: They are competent and have impact but probably through doing the things they are good at over and over, and doing them better and better. If this profile is like yours, the challenge for you is how to break out and develop a stronger meaning system so you want to take initiative to keep the system fresh and growing.

The internal and external profiles are illustrated in Figures 3.10 and 3.11. They are the mirror images of each other. "Internals" emphasize meaning and competence, whereas "externals" emphasize self-determination and impact. Internals are focused on feeling confident and feeling a connection to the organization, but with little action or impact. In contrast, externals are focused on having autonomy and impact but with little reflection on purpose or personal skill development. If either of these profiles resembles yours, the challenge for you is to become better

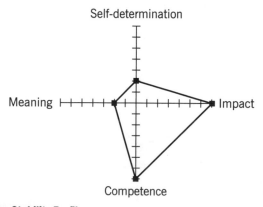

Figure 3.9. The Stability Profile

able to look both internally and externally, like the two-headed Roman god Janus, who looks simultaneously in two directions.

The last profile we discuss is illustrated in Figure 3.12. This rather rare profile is what we call the disempowered profile. This person scores relatively low on all four dimensions. This is not a very stable profile, particularly in terms of the low score on competence. Over time in any position, people typically build at least a moderate competence to do the job or they are replaced or choose a new position where they can feel at least moderately competent.

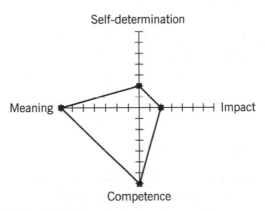

Figure 3.10. The Internal Profile

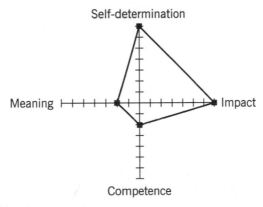

Figure 3.11. The External Profile

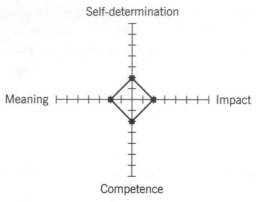

Figure 3.12. The Disempowered Profile

Looking at the shape of your empowerment profile enables you to identify specific areas to strengthen. Next we turn to how your scores on the various dimensions, and your overall level of empowerment, compare to those of others.

Benchmarking Your Level of Empowerment

So how empowered are you? To benchmark your level of empowerment in comparison to thousands of individuals who have completed the Psychological Empowerment Instrument, see Table 3.1. The table shows the percentile scores for individuals across a number of industries, including automotive, aerospace, insurance, computers, and financial services. The scores are for frontline U.S. and Asian employees all the way up to the executive ranks of the organization. We have provided some norms for each of the four dimensions of empowerment as well as the overall level of empowerment across all of these respondents. For example, consider the following scores:

- A 4.50 score on meaning puts you in the lowest 10 percent of people taking the PEI
- A 6.95 score on competence puts you in the highest 10 percent of people taking the PEI

- A 5.67 score on self-determination puts you in the middle 50 percent of people taking the PEI
- A 4.50 score on impact puts you in the lowest 40 percent of people taking the PEI
- A 5.82 score on overall empowerment puts you above 65 percent of people taking the PEI

These scores would indicate that you are doing very well in terms of the competence dimension, that there is great room for improvement on the meaning dimension, and that you are relatively weak on the self-determination and impact dimensions. Now see where you fall on each of your four dimensions of empowerment plus your overall empowerment score.

Table 3.1. Percentile Scores for Empowerment

Percentile	Meaning	Competence	Self-determination	Impact	Empowerment
Lowest 5%	3.67	4.33	3.67	2.00	4.17
10%	4.67	4.50	4.33	2.67	4.50
15%	4.80	4.75	4.67	3.00	4.69
20%	5.00	5.00	4.75	3.33	4.83
25%	5.25	5.25	4.85	3.67	5.00
30%	5.33	5.33	5.00	4.00	5.08
35%	5.50	5.51	5.30	4.33	5.19
40%	5.67	5.67	5.33	4.67	5.33
45%	5.75	5.71	5.50	4.82	5.42
50%	5.91	5.75	5.67	5.00	5.50
55%	6.00	5.82	5.72	5.03	5.58
60%	6.11	6.00	5.75	5.33	5.67
65%	6.22	6.25	5.93	5.50	5.81
70%	6.33	6.33	6.00	5.67	5.88
75%	6.50	6.50	6.08	5.78	6.00
80%	6.67	6.67	6.33	6.00	6.08
85%	6.78	6.75	6.38	6.35	6.19
90%	6.89	6.91	6.67	6.50	6.38
Highest 95%	7.00	7.00	7.00	7.00	6.58

To help you compare yourself with similar others, Figure 3.13 shows the average profiles from the thousands of people who have taken the Psychological Empowerment Instrument. This will give you a sense for what the profiles look like for various groups of people in different industries and cultures. It is interesting that there is some consistency across the profiles. In most cases, people tend to score highest on the competence dimension and to score lowest on the impact dimension. This indicates that people feel fairly confident that they have the skills and abilities necessary to do their work but that their work has limited impact on the larger system or unit of which they are a part.

■ How Can You Develop Your Own Sense of Empowerment?

You have now taken the PEI, profiled your score, and benchmarked yourself against the thousands of others who have completed this assessment. What have you learned?

 Take a few minutes to respond to the following questions in your empowerment journal:

- How do you feel about your overall level of empowerment?
- Which dimension are you most satisfied with?
  Why do you feel that you scored this way on this dimension? What sorts of things have facilitated your relatively good score on this dimension?
- Which dimension do you feel least satisfied with?
  Why do you feel that you scored this way on this dimension? What keeps you from feeling more empowered on this dimension?
- What have you learned so far that might help you sustain and build your level of empowerment?

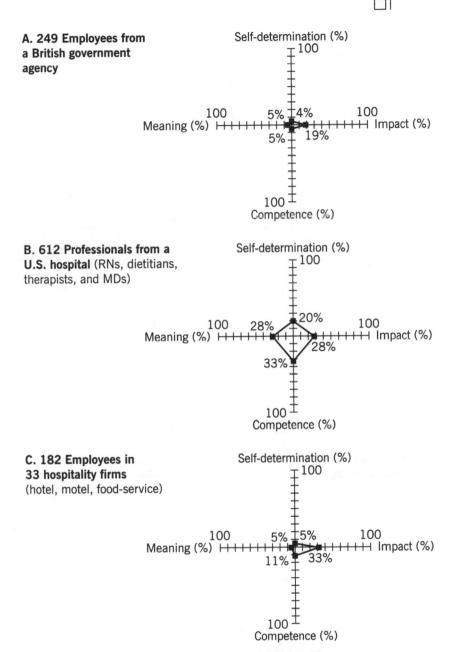

A. 249 Employees from a British government agency

Self-determination (%)
100
Meaning (%) — 100 — 5% 4% — 100 — Impact (%)
5% 19%
100
Competence (%)

B. 612 Professionals from a U.S. hospital (RNs, dietitians, therapists, and MDs)

Self-determination (%)
100
Meaning (%) — 100 — 28% 20% — 100 — Impact (%)
28%
33%
100
Competence (%)

C. 182 Employees in 33 hospitality firms (hotel, motel, food-service)

Self-determination (%)
100
Meaning (%) — 100 — 5% 5% — 100 — Impact (%)
11% 33%
100
Competence (%)

Figure 3.13. Profiles Across Industries, Levels, and Organizations

D. 544 Managers from an automotive company

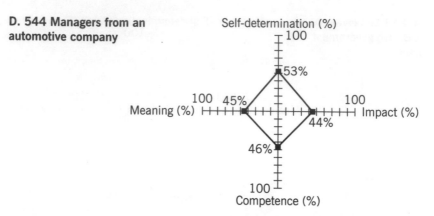

E. 128 Employees in an insurance company

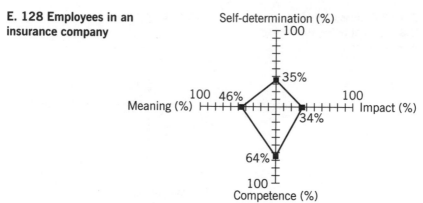

F. 183 Nurses in a community hospital

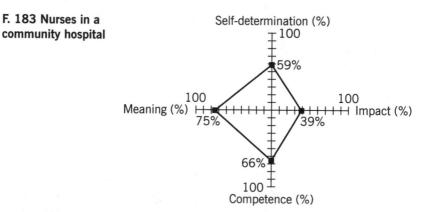

Figure 3.13. Profiles Across Industries, Levels, and Organizations, Cont'd

G. 279 Service employees in 30 private clubs

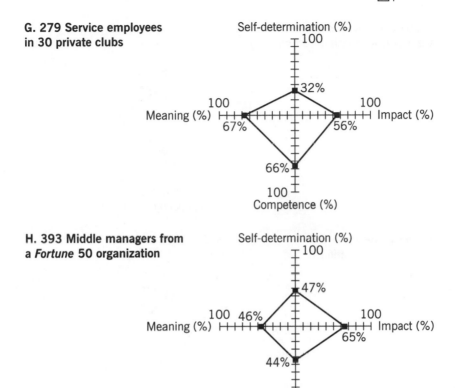

H. 393 Middle managers from a *Fortune* 50 organization

I. 98 Division managers from a global Asian electronics firm

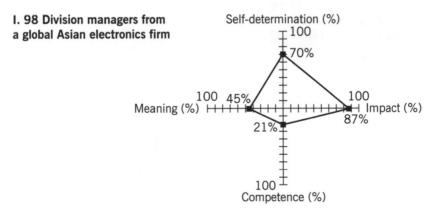

Figure 3.13. Profiles Across Industries, Levels, and Organizations, Cont'd

J. 157 Lower level managers from a global Asian electronics firm

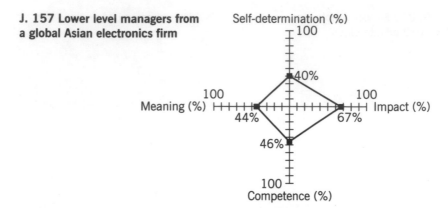

K. 348 Managers in an aerospace corporation

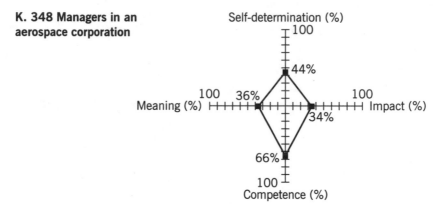

L. 786 Employees in an aerospace corporation

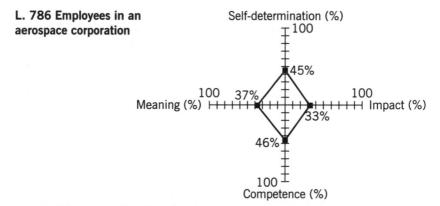

Figure 3.13. Profiles Across Industries, Levels, and Organizations, Cont'd

Sources: The figures are drawn from data provided as follows: A from Geelmuyden, M., and Silvester, E. "Empowerment in Government Services in the United Kingdom." Working paper, 1999; B from Koberg, C. S., Boss, R. W., Senjem, J. C., and Goodman, E. A. "Antecedents and Outcomes of Empowerment." Group and Organization Management, 1999, 24(1), 71–91; C from Sparrowe, R. T., "Empowerment in the Hospitality Industry: An Exploration of Antecedents and Outcomes." *Hospitality Research Journal*, 1994, *17*(3), 51–73; D from Spreitzer, G. M., Xin, K., and Perttula, K. H. "A Cultural Analysis of the Effectiveness of Transformational Leadership." Paper presented at the National Academy of Management meetings, Toronto, Canada, August 8–11, 2000; E from Spreitzer, G. M., "Psychological Empowerment in the Workplace: Dimensions, Measurement, and Validation." *Academy of Management Journal*, 1995, *38*(5), 1442–1468; F from Kraimer, M. C., Seibert, S. E., and Linden, R. C. "Psychological Empowerment as a Multidimensional Construct: A Test of Construct Validity." *Educational and Psychological Measurement*, 1997, *59*, 127–142; G from Fulford, M. D., and Enz, C. A. "The Impact of Empowerment on Service Employees." *Journal of Managerial Issues*, 1995, *7*(2), 161175; H from Spreitzer, G. M. "Social-Structural Characteristics of Psychological Empowerment." *Academy of Management Journal*, 1996, *39*(2), 483–504; I and J from Spreitzer, G. M., Xin, K., and Perttula, K. H. "A Cultural Analysis of the Effectiveness of Transformational Leadership." Paper presented at the National Academy of Management meetings, Toronto, Canada, August 8–11, 2000; K and L from Mishra, K., Spreitzer, G. M., and Mishra, A. "Preserving Employee Morale During Downsizing." *Sloan Management Review*, 1998, *39*(2), 83–95.

After you have had a chance to reflect on what you learned, the next question is, Where do you begin to increase your own empowerment? The remainder of this chapter offers specific suggestions for how to increase your level of self-determination, meaning, competence, and impact. You may find that you desire improvement on each of the dimensions, or you may find that you want to start out by focusing your energy on a single dimension.

Nurturing Meaning

This dimension is all about your identity as a person. "Purpose has to do with one's call—deciding what business you are in as a person."[5]

Richard Leider is a philosopher and consultant who focuses on helping clients build purpose.[6] At the heart of his approach is a belief that each individual is born with a reason for being and that life is a quest to discover that purpose. Have you discovered what your purpose is? Have you even begun to look for it? Too often we live life just one day at a time with little sense of what our long-term vision or legacy is—of the purpose of our being. The meaning dimension of empowerment involves a pilgrimage to seek such purpose. Let's begin your pilgrimage for meaning.

Many people find meaning in a sense of calling. We often think that a calling is something that applies only to religious life. But a sense of calling is the heart of empowerment, whether in a workplace context or elsewhere. If meaning is missing, we have little reason to commit ourselves to the work of the organization; we will merely go through the motions. Unfortunately, too many of us find our calling only outside the workplace through our families, volunteer work, or church life. Too often we view *life* as what we *choose* to do on the weekends, and *work* as what we *have* to do to be able to live out our lives. But when we align a personal calling with our work, we create a very powerful sense of meaning.

We can find exemplars of this sense of meaning in dedicated leaders like Mahatma Gandhi.[7] By his early forties, Gandhi had come to feel terror at the prospect of living to old age in conventional comfort. He trembled when he imagined himself on his deathbed uttering the most tragic of all last words: "I could have done much more with my life." Instead, he embraced the challenge of fighting for the independence of India from British imperialism. For the next forty years, he focused all his energies on this ambitious goal. Notice that Gandhi came upon the work that provided meaning midway through life. It is never too late to begin the quest.

What can meaning look like in a business context? For Jack Welch, CEO of GE, it meant taking an already successful company and leading it toward its full potential by transforming it to become the world's most competitive company. For Gil Whitaker and Joe White, two successive deans of the Michigan Business School, it meant taking an already good business school and transforming it into a world-class institution. For us, it has meant spreading a message through our research and teaching to students and executives that they can make a difference in creating a better workplace. Earlier in our careers, our focus was on more mundane things like publishing our work in the right journals, getting the best teaching ratings, and gaining tenure and promotion. But these are not the sort of things that energize people. They create technical skill and predictable outputs but not purpose.

 Take a few quiet moments now to think about your own sense of meaning. Here are some questions to guide you. Be honest with yourself:

- Who am I?
- What do I want to be? What is my legacy?
- How do I want to get there?
- Am I on the right track?
- What is keeping me from being all that I want to be?
- What I can do to overcome these barriers to meaning?

Courses of Action

The questions just listed can help you diagnose the kind of direction you have in your life. If you want more sense of meaning and purpose in your work life, consider the following set of activities.

1. *Take time for reflection.* Too often we get caught up fighting the day-to-day fires that inevitably creep into our lives: the end-of-the-year report we need to finish, the problem customer who just can't be pleased, the care needed by our children or our elderly parents, our commitments to our volunteer activities or church group. All of these things deserve our time, but they can block out the kind of long-term focus that is so important for meaning. They can also burn us out. Remember to take time out of your busy schedule to reflect and think about the big picture of what you ultimately want out of life.

Ideally, this time for reflection would be the kind of paid sabbatical that academic environments provide and that many high-tech firms are beginning to offer. But this may not be an option for you. If this is the case, you need to carve out time for your own sabbatical. This might mean taking a day every six months just for yourself where you won't be disturbed with a ringing phone or beeping e-mail so you can think strategically about your purpose and mission. It might mean making an appointment with yourself for the first couple hours of work time every other Friday to keep a journal of your thoughts, feelings, and aspirations. If you don't make time for these sorts of activities, it's too easy to focus on getting through today without thinking about what comes next. When will you schedule an appointment with yourself?

2. *Identify your special gifts and talent.* This is an excellent way to begin your sabbatical. Take a few minutes and write down what you think makes you a truly unique human being. What can you do better than almost anyone you know? This is your source of competitive advantage.

As an example, consider the case of the computer salesman who recognized that he was extraordinarily talented at connecting with older people and building their trust. This was a group that the company had not targeted in its marketing efforts. This salesman realized that by using his talent he could help open up the Internet world to older people who were isolated in their homes. Rather than just selling his product and opening a larger new market, he would be helping these people to find a connection in the new electronic age. He could build their trust and help them feel comfortable with this new technology.

How can you align your work with your true source of competitive advantage to make the best use of your special gifts and talents?

3. *Write your obituary.* What will your legacy be? To focus on this question, write your own obituary. Morbid though this sounds, this exercise forces us to think about what we most want to be remembered for. Will we be like Gandhi in his forties and say, "I wish I had done more," or even worse, "I wish I had done

something different"? As the old saying goes, "You can't take it with you." Or as a newer saying has it, "I never saw a U-haul following a hearse." What do you want to leave behind for the next generation to remember you by and thank you for?

4. *Write your own life mission statement.* There are several parts to this exercise. First, discover what moves you. Where do you find joy? What truly makes you happy? What kinds of activities are so effortless for you that you lose a sense of time?

Second, think hard about where you want to go. What is your life vision? Articulate your vision in a simple paragraph.

Third, how do you want to get there? What are the core values that will guide you? What sacrifices are you willing to make to achieve your vision? What sacrifices are you *not* willing to make?

Action Planning

Developing real meaning is not a simple process. It takes deep introspection. It means we have to make ourselves vulnerable by identifying what we are really all about. These things don't take days—they take a lifetime. But there is no better time than the present to get started.

 In your empowerment journal, list three specific actions aimed at increasing your sense of meaning that you are prepared to commit to.

Developing Greater Competence

Ironically, the one sure way to build our confidence and capability is continually to stretch ourselves in new ways and learn new things. "Just like fruit on a tree, when we stop growing, we start to rot."[8] We build our competence by making ourselves vulnerable to new ways of doing and being. If we don't stretch, we tend to get stale. Staleness leads us to question our ability, and our confidence suffers.

To better understand this irony, consider how the recent explosion of the Internet has affected professors. Since the late 1990s, it has been impossible to pick up a copy of a popular business periodical and not see some story about how the Internet is taking over the world we live in—from shopping to entertainment to education. For teachers, the potential transformation of the educational system is downright threatening. Why should students drive an hour to class when they can take the same course via the Internet in their living room or office? We may have to entirely rethink how we deliver education. We may now have to teach students through distance learning rather than in case rooms. But this is not the medium of the master teacher, is it? Real learning comes from face-to-face classroom discussions, doesn't it? Our natural tendency is to resist this new teaching approach, but our confidence will only improve when we embrace it, learn the new perspective, and grow.

But an even more onerous implication for us is that the content of what we teach and what we research may be becoming outmoded in the Internet age. We've been through more than one hallway conversation in which professors are digging their heads into the sand, denying that the Internet is having any substantive impact on the way we should manage our people, market and design our products, build relationships with our customers and suppliers, or control our finances. Are we kidding ourselves? The virtual world is changing all these things in significant ways. Instead of seeing this newness as a source of threat, we must reframe it as a source of opportunity, a source of learning and growth. To remain a master teacher, we must transform ourselves to respond to the age of the Internet by changing and growing ourselves.

How many people in other kinds of organizations suffer from similar false assumptions and self-delusions when they are faced with significant change? We all want to stay in our comfort zones, but we all need continually to renew ourselves. Building our competence means making ourselves vulnerable to finding out that our theories, our models, or our assumptions may not apply or may work differently in a new environment. It means stretching ourselves and challenging our ways of being to make our former selves obsolete. This continual renewal is an important component of empowerment.

 Here is a set of questions you might use to guide you in developing your personal sense of mastery:

- In what ways do I make myself vulnerable by learning from and adapting to the changing business environment?
- Do I seek out new opportunities for training and development or do I wait until I am told to attend a training program?
- In what ways do I stretch myself in new ways on a regular basis? Provide two examples from the last month.
- Do I regularly invest in books, seminars, and conferences to expose myself to new ways of thinking about my work?
- What could I do to be known in my department for keeping up to date on the newest, most cutting-edge ideas in my field?

Courses of Action

If your response to any of these questions indicates room for improvement, you may find the following set of tools helpful in developing your sense of competence.

1. *Become a disciplined reader.* Skim popular business periodicals weekly to keep abreast of new trends and developments. Subscribe to *Fast Company,* a relatively new monthly publication, that prides itself on being on the cutting edge (take a look, even its format is different). Visit a local bookstore on a regular basis to peruse its collection of business books or books relevant to your specific field. At a minimum, commit to reading one new book per month to keep abreast of new ways of thinking. Ask

friends who you think are particularly creative or thoughtful for recommendations. Look for reviews of influential books in popular business outlets such as *Business Week, Fortune,* or the *Wall Street Journal.*

2. *Expose yourself to industry groups.* Industry groups have local chapters in most urban areas. They also sponsor regional meetings to bring industry experts together to share knowledge. Although these groups aren't always on the cutting edge in terms of new ideas, they will give you important exposure outside your organization to help you keep up with emerging trends. They will also help you form important networks and build your social capital.

3. *Return to school for a check-up.* Most business schools offer continuing education for people at all levels of an organization—from senior managers to first-level supervisors. Don't wait for your company to tell you to attend a program; instead, adopt a mindset of lifelong learning. School is not just about getting a degree; it's also about learning how to learn over the course of a lifetime. Returning to campus every few years for a refresher will help keep you exposed to new ideas and approaches to your work. (Many companies pay the tuition for employees.) Going back to school will also give you the break that is often needed for personal reflection and breakthrough ideas. It can be a minisabbatical that refreshes and energizes you.

4. *Keep your resume up to date and your eyes open for new job opportunities.* Keeping your resume up to date will help you think about your know-how and skill set. Do your skills and capabilities meet the needs of today's changing business environment, or do you feel yourself becoming obsolete? Give your resume a test run and apply for a new job now and then, whether within or outside your company. This exercise will provide you with important information on your employability. Who knows, you might even find yourself in a new position. And there is nothing like a new position to stretch yourself, learn, and grow in new

ways. If you get a lukewarm response on your employability, this may indicate that it is time for some stretch and updating.

Action Planning
Competence is something we must work at daily to keep ourselves at the cutting edge. Remember, competence isn't about what you already know how to do well; it's about continually stretching yourself.

 In your empowerment journal, describe three specific actions aimed at stretching yourself that you are prepared to commit to.

Increasing Self-Determination

Ask forgiveness rather than seek permission. So often in organizations, it is more comfortable to wait to take action until someone tells us what to do than it is to take initiative. This is the foundation of command-and-control management—the essence of traditional hierarchical systems. Those at the top have the answers to direct those below them. As a result, over time, organizations have conditioned employees *not* to take initiative because they might be wrong—they might make a mistake, they might fail.

We learn to find comfort in this command-and-control system because if a mistake is made, we aren't responsible for it—someone else told us what to do. In this way we learn to avoid initiative and kick difficult decisions up to the boss. After all, why would any reasonable person want to be held accountable for a decision that might turn out to be wrong or unpopular?

But what happens when the world we live in gets too complex for those at the top to have all of the answers? In today's world, those at the front line often have more knowledge and information to make decisions than those at the top. Those on the front lines are the ones interacting with the customer, service, or product. They know where the problems are and often have solutions for them. Clearly, today's organizations need employees who are willing to take initiative, although they aren't always ready to admit it. So the question becomes, how do we learn to take initiative?

 How autonomous are you willing to be? The following questions should provide fodder for thought about your level of self-determination.

- In what ways do I act autonomously? What are counterexamples in which I wait for others to direct me?
- When I am asked to take initiative or solve a problem, do I try to kick the problem back to my boss?
- When I have made a mistake in the past, have I put the blame on someone else—have I used the excuse that someone told me what to do? What could I do differently regarding future mistakes?

Courses of Action

If your answer to any of the questions just listed suggests room for personal growth, refer to the following set of tips and techniques for continuously developing your sense of autonomy.

1. *Create small wins.* Often we become overwhelmed with what we think it means to take action. We become paralyzed because we do not know where to begin. A number of years ago, Karl Weick, a faculty member at the University of Michigan, coined the term *small wins* to help us overcome this natural paralysis. Rather than undertaking extremely ambitious initiatives that are likely to be overwhelming and may generate significant resistance, Weick argues that we should start with small, attainable goals that when achieved will help generate momentum and build our courage and competence.

To illustrate: A few years ago, a department head decided that he wanted to change the focus of the department. His initial intuition was that he should make his vision public, recommend a name change for the department, and implement a new performance management system. But he quickly realized that this kind of change would generate significant resistance. Instead, he decided that the next person the department would hire would be someone who would epitomize his new vision. This was within his control and would generate little opposition but would help build some momentum toward his goal. Over several months, he made several strategic hires, and a few other faculty members left due to natural attrition. The department chair had now achieved a significant mass of faculty in the department who would support the new vision. In fact, there was so much momentum for the new vision that a member of the department who the chair initially believed would be resistant to the change actually suggested a name change for the department to reflect its recent shift—all without the department chair saying a word about a new direction for the group.

Small wins, then, are the baby steps that help us get moving in the right direction. They get us past paralysis—and before long, we're not just walking, we're running.

2. *Learn from your mistakes.* Nothing ventured, nothing gained. But to venture is to take a risk. If we're always afraid we'll fail, we will probably never try. But if we believe that failure is an important mechanism for learning, we won't be so concerned about making a mistake.

Research has shown that most of us fail initially when we try something new, but real leaders persevere in learning from their mistakes and then move forward. In fact, some of the best ideas emerge from mistakes. For example, the sticky substance used on Post-It Notes was the result of a failed experiment at 3M to create a glue with a low level of tackiness. The substance that was created was so untacky that it couldn't really be considered glue. This failure turned into one of the most popular (and enduring) new products of the 1980s.

3. *JDI, but DBS.* Several years ago, the University of Michigan partnered with the Ford Motor Company to develop a leadership development program aimed at empowering middle managers. One motto that emerged during the program was a take-off on Nike's catch-phrase, "Just do it," or JDI. The idea was to get people to take initiative and act as owners of the firm rather than waiting for someone to tell them what to do. But some managers responded by saying that some high-risk initiatives would be paramount to professional suicide. The group eventually changed the letters to "JDI but DBS": Just do it, but don't be stupid.

4. *Push against your boundaries.* Clearly, you need to be politically sensitive to what the boundaries of your initiative are. But our sense is that most people are much more cautious than they need to be. Most boundaries are much more permeable than we think. If you don't get pushed back now and then, you probably aren't pushing hard enough.

Action Planning

Gaining autonomy means being willing to take initiative. It means not kicking difficult decisions back up the organizational hierarchy and not being lulled by the comfort of accepting direction.

 In your empowerment journal, describe three specific actions aimed at taking initiative that you are prepared to commit to.

Increasing Impact

Whereas self-determination focuses on the act of taking initiative, impact focuses on the magnitude of the initiative we undertake. In other words, impact has to do with undertaking influential initiatives—ones that involve significant change and real innovation—as opposed to "continual improvement" initiatives that merely make incremental improvements on the existing system. Having impact means making such a powerful difference that the system wouldn't be the same without your action.

Having an impact often requires "walking naked into the land of uncertainty." It involves stepping outside well-defined boundaries with the very real possibility of failure but also the hope of a breakthrough idea. Taking this kind of initiative requires courage. It means putting ourselves on the line. It is risky because mistakes are inevitable, especially when we are just learning. But not daring to have an impact means we that we check our brains at the door. It means that our ideas never see the light of day.

It is all too easy to pursue the slow death strategy of using our hard-earned competencies within the status quo, staying within our comfort zone. But choosing empowerment means "building the bridge as we walk on it"–initiating deep change before we even understand it or know what the solution is. We only find the solution once we engage in the process.

 Do you have the courage to make a real difference? The following questions should provide some material for reflection.

- How do I fail to risk deep change and inadvertently accept slow death?
- Reflect on one example of when I had the courage to do what I thought was right.
- Would my organization be the same without me, or do I make a real difference? How?

Courses of Action
If you are like most of us, reading about the *impact* dimension sends shivers down your spine. Daring to have impact is terrifying. It means real vulnerability. It requires engaging uncertainty

and ambiguity. It means taking a risk. How in the world do we do this without committing professional suicide? Here are some ideas.

1. *Think outside the box.* Having an impact means getting outside the tried and true way of doing things to try something really new. Brainstorming is often a good way to start. Without any feasibility analyses, take a problem you are experiencing in the workplace, and come up with at least thirty solutions. More is better because more leads to divergent thinking. Don't be afraid to be outrageous. Ask others for their ideas, even others who aren't part of your context, people you know from other domains of life such as from your family, your church. New ideas often come from outside the system.

2. *Sell the issue.* Making an impact means making sure that others understand and buy into your ideas. The best idea is only an idea if it can't be implemented. Whereas innovation requires divergence of thinking, getting the innovation accepted requires convergence in terms of gaining acceptance and support. You might achieve this convergence by convincing others of the benefits of your idea by persuading them with a compelling vision. Probably you need to secure sponsorship from powerful others who support you even if they don't fully understand your idea. And you probably need to model the kind of changes you are advocating so that others can see how they work. All this can take time. The more radical the change you propose, the more persistent you may need to be in getting people to give it a try. If you let yourself become discouraged the first time you hear "no," your brilliant brainchild may be stillborn. The point is, coming up with innovative ideas isn't enough. To have impact, you must find ways to make sure your ideas get accepted and implemented.

3. *Trust yourself.* To have real impact, you must have the courage to trust yourself. If you can't trust yourself, who can you trust? Often we second guess ourselves, wondering whether we have what it takes. Too many times, we see someone else come up with a breakthrough solution that has real impact, and we

think, I thought of that a long time ago. But thinking about something is not enough to have impact. Trusting in ourselves means learning to follow our intuition, rely on our hunches, listen to our sixth sense—and risk taking action.

Action Planning
Making an impact means having the courage to seek initiative. It means making ourselves vulnerable by doing what we think is right now and not just doing what has always been done in the past. In short, impact requires us to take risks.

 In your empowerment journal, describe three specific actions aimed at developing the courage to make a real difference that you are prepared to commit to.

CHAPTER SUMMARY
This chapter focuses on the first discipline of empowerment: empowering ourselves. Before we can expect others to become empowered—to act as leaders—we must empower ourselves. So before worrying about how to change the system around us, we must first look inward.

After reading this chapter, you should have a clear sense of your own level of empowerment on each of the four dimensions: self-determination, meaning, impact, and competence. After completing your empowerment profile and benchmarking yourself against the thousands of others who have completed the assessment, you have a good sense of your personal strengths and weaknesses. Very few of us have a fully empowered profile with high scores on each dimension. The challenge is how to develop the dimensions where we have lower scores.

The reflection questions in the final section of the chapter can help you diagnose the reasons for your weaknesses so that you can address them directly. We have encouraged you to commit to specific courses of action to improve each dimension you choose to work on. Once you begin to realize more of your own empowerment potential, you can turn to the other disciplines of empowerment, which focus on developing a climate that fosters leadership behavior.

The Second Discipline
Continuous Vision and Challenge

As we have emphasized throughout this book, we cannot create a company of leaders by directly empowering others. What we *can* do is create an environment that increases the probability that people will choose to empower themselves. As we discussed in the preceding chapter, the first key element in that environment of leadership is you and me. Only if we empower ourselves can we expect those around us to choose to empower themselves. And once we have empowered ourselves we provide a model for them. We can then further increase the probability that they will empower themselves by practicing the four remaining disciplines of empowerment.

The next discipline of empowerment is *continuous vision and challenge*. Consider the following scenario:

An executive at a large chemical company (let's call him Sam) wanted his people to be leaders. He seemed to be doing everything right: He offered training in self-management, shared sensitive information about the business, and rewarded people for the extra responsibility they were taking on.

Initially, there was a lot of enthusiasm about empowerment. But almost immediately, when people had a decision to make, they would come to Sam to ask, "Is this what you wanted? Is this right?" He would send them away, telling them, "Remember, you are empowered, I trust you to make the decision yourself." Some people at this point would reiterate, "But I don't know what you want." Others would reluctantly go away and make the decision, but it was often the "wrong" decision—one that would take the organization off course. After several weeks of this, Sam decided that his people just weren't ready for empowerment.

 Why didn't empowerment take at Sam's company? Before reading further, take a minute to jot down your diagnosis in your empowerment journal.

Why did Sam's well-intentioned effort to create empowerment fail? We think that the people did not know where the unit was going—they did not have a vision. If we asked the people what it was like to work there they would have said things like this: "In this unit there is a reluctance to make decisions. We do not know where we are supposed to be going. It is easy to make mistakes when you do not know what is wanted." When people don't know where the unit is going, they're going to be uncomfortable making their own decisions. Without a compass to guide them, they won't know whether their decisions will be aligned with where the organization needs to go. As a result, they may not connect to the strategy. And if they do take the initiative to make a decision, they are likely to guess wrong and make a decision that won't help the organization achieve its vision.

Sam may have had his own sense of where he wanted to take the organization, but the behavior of his employees suggests that he never communicated a compelling vision or strategy. Was the vision to be on the cutting edge of new production technology? Was it to become more global? Was it to create the most advanced chemical compounds through intensive R&D? Depending on what the vision for the company was, the criteria of what constituted a good decision would look very different. If, for example, Sam had clearly articulated a vision of becoming more global, his people would have sensed the appropriate decision in choosing between allocating capital expenditures to move into a new country versus adopting a new technology, or between investing new monies in R&D versus marketing current products in new territories. Sam's people were reluctant to make decisions because they weren't clear whether this, or something else, was the vision for the organization.

The connection between vision and empowered action should be clear. A *vision* provides the direction people need to take initiative confidently and intelligently, without waiting for permission from top management. It helps them keep their eye on the ball and set clear priorities even in the absence of direct supervision. In our research, highly empowered people report that they understand and feel challenged and inspired by top management's vision for the organization: They know the company's strategic direction.

Vision is thus the first requirement in creating a context in which people can act in empowered ways. This chapter explores how to create a compelling vision that challenges people to stretch and realize their potential as leaders.

■ What Is Vision?

Vision comes from the Latin root *visus,* "to see." To have a vision
is to see clearly where the organization intends to go. Beyond clar-
ity, a vision fosters leadership behavior if it is challenging enough
to require employees to stretch and exciting enough to energize
them. President John F. Kennedy articulated this kind of vision
for NASA in the 1960s: "to put a man on the moon by the end of
this decade." The vision was clearly and simply stated, and it was
highly challenging. No one really knew whether Kennedy's ambitious goal could be reached in such a short window of time. If
the goal was achievable—and events proved that it was—it was
near the limit of what people could reasonably attempt.

This clear and inspiring vision was so engrained in NASA
employees that if you were to ask the janitor or cafeteria cashier
what their job was, they would probably answer, "putting a man
on the moon." Similarly, the Catholic Archdiocese in Los Angeles currently is building what church leaders call "the cathedral
for the new millennium" to replace the one that was badly dam-
aged in the 1994 Northridge earthquake. The vision is to build
a cathedral that will last, not a hundred years as the current one
did, but a thousand years. This vision requires an entirely different mentality from the one that built the original church, and
it pervades the craft of each worker on the project. If you ask any
worker, from the architect to the bricklayer, what the purpose of
his or her work is, the answer is likely to be the same: "to build
a cathedral that can stand for a thousand years." From the ma-
terials to the craftsmanship, this vision establishes clear priorities that focus the work on quality and longevity. Moreover, it
inspires people to give their best effort. Everyone associated
with the project knows that their work will create an important
legacy for the generations who will celebrate masses, baptisms,
weddings, and funerals in this structure.

Locating Vision in the Empowerment Model

The discipline of vision is focused on the future, with an orientation toward flexibility and change rather than the status quo. It is consistent with the blend of the mechanistic and organic perspectives on empowerment discussed in Chapter Two because it emphasizes the need for direction while trusting people to take initiative. If you return for a moment to Figure 2.1, which depicts the framework of empowerment disciplines, you will notice that vision appears in the upper right-hand quadrant. This quadrant is in creative tension with the security quadrant in the lower left-hand part of the model. Whereas the security quadrant emphasizes building comfort zones and support for employees, the vision quadrant focuses on stretching people and moving them in new directions.

Assessing Your Vision

As with self-empowerment, the place to begin in strengthening the discipline of vision is to assess where you are now.

 Imagine that you were assigned to report on your organization's vision in a meeting with your department or management team. In your empowerment journal, write down what you would say. Don't check any sources, just write from memory.

What did you write down? If you are like a lot of people, you may have had trouble coming up with a succinct statement of the vision for the organization—a sure sign of trouble. Or perhaps you wrote out a formal statement of the company's vision that has been distributed to you and others on a plastic card. Although there is nothing wrong with emblazoning the corporate vision on such aids, empowered individuals are likely to express a unique vision for their own unit that supports the corporate direction. The vision isn't something they carry in their pockets; it's something they live by day to day. It is embedded in their hearts and minds because it is the foundation that underlies what they do. Ask any one of the 99,000 employees who work at Johnson & Johnson what their vision is, and they will tell you that their first responsibility is to the doctors, nurses, patients, mothers, and fathers who use their products and services— products and services that people can trust.

This kind of shared vision animates the personal vision that each employee needs in order to act as a leader. Yet even such a shared vision is probably not enough. Clear vision needs to exist at every level of the organization. To illustrate:

We once worked with the senior management team of a *Fortune* 500 company. The CEO turned to one of his direct reports and asked, "What is your vision statement?" The person became very flustered. He stated, "The vision is not my job, it is yours." The CEO made no comment but called on each of the others present. They all struggled. The CEO then said, "If you have no vision for your particular business, then how can you lead your business?"

Taking the CEO's point one step further, we have had many conversations with managers who say that it is impossible to have a vision for their own units because unlike the people in the preceding story, their company has provided no corporate vision. We tell them that this is justifying one's own sin with the sin of the boss. If we are to lead, we must provide those we lead with a vision. Many managers respond by saying that coming up with their own visions would produce chaos.

But where top management has not articulated a clear vision, the chaos already exists. Within our own realm of responsibility, we still need to call forth a common mindset. Moreover, if we formulate our own vision, we not only help our people, but we also challenge the boss to create a vision for the organization as a whole.

The ideal, of course, is to have a vision at every level that coheres with the overall vision for the organization. Ask the 14,000 employees of the Ritz-Carlton about their vision, and they will ask you whether you are interested in the overall company vision statement, their property's vision statement, or their personal vision statement. Though these visions will differ in detail, they will all be variations on a single theme. All will revolve around one overarching mission: to be the premier luxury hotel chain around the world by offering "surprise and delight" service to every customer. Says Horst Schulze, president and chief operating officer of the Ritz-Carlton: "Every employee has the business plan of the Ritz-Carlton in his or her pocket, constantly reinforcing that guest satisfaction is our highest mission." The corporate vision is the umbrella that holds the vision statements of the units and their people.

We recently tested this claim at the Ritz. We asked our van driver what his vision was. He told us he was the head of the vanpool and showed us the vision statement for his local facility. Then he said his vision was to create the best transportation support system in the world and that every one of his drivers was committed to doing so. He described how even the vanpool was critical to the Ritz-Carlton to achieve its overall vision.

So how do you create a vision that fosters empowerment, one that facilitates a sense of ownership and energizes people to give their best? The answer involves both the *content* of your vision and the *process* by which the vision is created.

■ The Content of an Empowering Vision

In our research, we have found that a vision encourages leadership behavior if it meets three criteria: it evokes passion, it challenges employees to stretch and grow, and it provides a sense of legacy.

Passion

Empowerment requires faith and hope in the future. It is the antithesis of fatalism or cynicism. Consequently, a vision can facilitate empowerment only if it grabs, excites, and energizes. An empowering vision is compelling to employees; it expresses a worthwhile purpose they can believe in, and it invites them to perceive new possibilities.

Consider the vision of a financial services company: "Making customers' dreams come true." This is a vision employees can feel passionate about; it is more compelling than a more mundane vision focused on making money or increasing market share. Similarly, Disney has a vision that focuses on "Creating memories." Whether people are at a theme park, on a Disney cruise, or watching a Disney movie for the first time, the aim is to make it a special moment. This is a vision that anyone with children or anyone who was once a child can relate to.

These kinds of vision build *meaning*. They give employees a reason to *want* to be part of the organization and thereby solidify the personal connection to the organization, its products, and its services.

Challenge

To encourage empowerment, a vision needs to push the outside of the envelope by inviting employees to stretch themselves to the limits of their potential. A sign of a challenging vision is that it leaves people wondering, "Can we really accomplish this? I'm not sure—but if we do, it will be a *real* breakthrough, something that has never been accomplished before." When President Kennedy articulated the vision for NASA, it was not clear whether the United States could develop the technology and expertise to put a man on the moon within ten years. The drive to meet this ambitious goal and to win the race to the moon with the Soviet Union prompted employees to work extremely hard, persist in the face of setbacks, and sustain their energy. Recall, too, that it is by stretching ourselves that we develop confidence and greater *competence*—one of the four dimensions of empowerment.

Consider the audacious vision of the March of Dimes when it was established by Franklin Roosevelt in 1938. The vision was to eradicate polio, a crippling disease that was storming the nation and had no cure. But with this vision, the organization was able to mobilize tremendous energy and resources, and the disease was virtually eradicated in just two decades. Rather than become obsolete itself, the organization evolved its vision to the eradication of all birth defects—another challenging goal.

Jack Welch was able to create an intense challenge at General Electric (GE) in the 1980s when he created the "rule of No. 1 or No. 2." That meant that any GE business that was not number one or two in its industry would be fixed, sold, or closed. Within a few years, housewares, TV sets, and cellular communications were no longer within the GE product line.[1] Imagine the challenge this created for GE general managers who had believed that as long as they were making their numbers, even if they were average in their industry, they were performing adequately.

Legacy

Finally, a vision invites empowerment when it not only evokes passion in the present but also connects with the desire to create a legacy for the future, to be part of something larger than oneself. Such a vision encourages people to broaden their focus from "What's in it for me?" to "What can I leave behind for those who come after me?" Gandhi, in his efforts to lead the independence movement in India, said it elegantly: "We must be the change we wish to see."[2] A focus on legacy helps people believe they can have a lasting *impact* by helping shape the future.

The vision of a "cathedral for a millennium" has this notion of legacy. The cathedral workers are creating a legacy for generations to come. True, your company may not have a vision that spans a thousand years. But there are other kinds of legacy that are just as meaningful. A good example is Ben and Jerry's, the ice cream maker. Their mission is dedicated to "the creation and demonstration of a new corporate concept of linked prosperity." Their product is not merely the scrumptious ice cream they are famous for. Their product is also the new kind of corporate entity that places social responsibility on the same plane as financial success. What a legacy to leave behind—a new concept for an organization. Even as their company was recently being acquired by Unilever, Ben Cohen and Jerry Greenfield held a forum on preserving their original corporate mission, including the donation of 7.5 percent of the company's pretax earnings to charitable causes.

 Revisit the vision statement you jotted down earlier. To what extent does your vision have an empowering content? Does it evoke passion? Does it challenge? Does it connect with a notion of legacy? If your answer is no to any of these questions, think about how your vision statement could be refreshed. What kind of vision would make you proud to be part of your organization? What kind of vision would create ownership for you? In your journal, write a new vision statement for your company that you believe will elicit passion, create challenge, and connect with the future and the common good.

■ The Process of an Empowering Vision

While the content of a vision is crucial, the process by which the vision is developed can have even more of an influence on creating a climate of empowerment. Unfortunately, many leaders use a process that limits empowerment.

The traditional textbook approach to creating a vision goes something like this:

- The leader develops a compelling vision
- The leader sells the vision to the organization to get buy-in
- The followers implement the vision following the leader's direction

Isn't it obvious that this process runs counter to the idea of encouraging empowered leadership in others? All too often a vision created unilaterally by the leader winds up being viewed as little more than nice words displayed on the wall or the company's Web page. A vision that is developed in this way has little impact because people don't have a sense of ownership of it. They might give it lip service at appropriate moments, but they aren't likely to be personally invested in it. Is this how your organization's vision was developed?

 What is the origin of your organization's vision statement? Write down in your empowerment journal, to the best of your recollection, how you came to be aware of the company vision. Analyze whether that process has enhanced your own feelings of empowerment.

Next, ask yourself what process you have used in creating a vision for your own unit. Do you think the process has led to feelings of ownership among the people you work with?

■ An Idealized Process

In addition to doing the research necessary for this book, we have been involved with several companies that have put visions in place. The process is never the same twice. Yet each time we learn something. Recently we were asked: "Given your experience, in the ideal, what would the process of an empowering vision look like?" We have been thinking about that very appropriate question. In answer we suggest the following scenario that is an amalgam of the best of what we have seen in several different companies:

A CEO (we'll call him John) was troubled. He realized that the current vision of the company had little life to it. It was a set of words on a plastic card. At the same time, his company was being bombarded by the competition, particularly dot-com start-ups. Though he kept it to himself, he secretly worried about the long-term survival of his company.

After talking to several CEO friends and a set of consultants, he decided it was time to instill some life and direction back into his company. It was time for a change, and that change needed to be guided by a vision—a direction for the future. His first impulse was to sit down in his office and write a new vision statement himself and then work on getting buy-in from his senior team and eventually employees at all levels of the organization. After all, isn't that the role of great leaders—to be visionary?

But he soon discovered that creating a compelling vision was not easy to do. As he struggled with this visioning process, serendipitously, a group of middle managers asked to meet with him. They told him that it was getting increasingly hard for the company to attract new business and that current accounts were being snatched up by the competition. The company's competitors were more nimble and were developing more Web-based applications that their customers seemed to want. The managers said that they worried about their company's long-term prospects.

John was tempted to try to reassure the group that he had foreseen this trend and had a strategy for getting the company on track. But it was a moment of truth for him. He realized that he didn't have what it would take to do this by himself. The world was too complex, there was too much uncertainty. In order to turn things around and build a compelling vision for the future, he would have to engage the minds and hearts of everyone in the organization. So he admitted to the group that he, too, was troubled by what he was seeing, but that he wasn't sure what the best strategy for combating this problem would be. He needed their help. They were to become the envisioning team and were given some release time from their current responsibilities to focus on this creation process.

Before sending them off, he reminded the managers of the core values that the company espoused: care for the customer, deep respect for employees, innovative products, and value to shareholders. He told them that they had freedom to determine the vision as long as they made sure that it was consistent with these values. He challenged them to develop a vision that would leave a legacy for the next generation of employees.

The middle managers came from across different parts of the organization, so the envisioning team was naturally cross-functional. Their first task was to collect as much data as they could about the current environment. The team members each went back to their units and held brainstorming sessions about how to address their current problems and what employees' expectations were of the future. They met with current customers, as well as those who had been lured away by the competition, to get a better sense for their expectations and needs. They shadowed customers to try to discover whether there were other needs of which the customers might not even be aware. They speculated about who might be their customers of the future. They talked to industry analysts about their assessment of the company and their insights on the future of the industry. They talked to technology experts about what innovations might be on the horizon.

Then the team members reassembled with all this information in hand. On one wall, they mapped out the current problems the organization was facing. They identified fifteen major issues ranging from a resistance to new technologies to an inability to attract and retain the best people. On another wall, they mapped out their expectations for the future.

Here they identified important trends ranging from "anytime-anywhere" information access to the potential for consolidation in their industry.

Finally, with these weeks of work behind them, the team members began to draft a vision statement. Their goal was to create a vision that would be simple, compelling, and energizing, one that would guide and inspire. After drafting a short paragraph, the middle managers went back to their units and asked for feedback from small groups of employees from all parts of the organization. Was the vision understandable? Was it compelling? Was it something they could commit to? Did it create a sense of legacy? They asked for recommendations for improvement. Then they came together to work through the feedback they had received. They rewrote the vision statement to clarify the parts that didn't make sense and to solidify a clearer identity for the company that would differentiate it from the competition.

The work didn't stop there. Once again the team members took the vision statement back to their people for yet another round of feedback. At the same time, the middle managers began to work with their own units to draft complementary vision statements. These unit vision statements also began to translate the vision into specific roles and goals that would bring meaning to those in the unit. What is especially important, the unit vision statements were not only aligned with the overall vision for the company, but they also addressed the specific issues, tasks, and identity of the unit. This iterative process helped personalize the vision for people and make it real to them. A vision comes alive when people can see how it links directly to them and how their actions can make a difference in making the vision a reality.

After the vision statement had been through this final round of revisions, the team brought it to John. This was the first time he saw it. At no point had John told the envisioning team to report back to him. He trusted that the team members had the capability and the commitment to create a vision to bring the organization back to life. When they presented their vision to him, he asked only two questions: Was this a vision they found compelling and were truly committed to? Was this a vision that reinforced the core values of the organization? Their affirmative answers were all John needed to accept the vision. He knew that the vision that emerged from this process was the will and inspiration of his people. They were committed to bringing the vision to fruition, and they did.

This idealized visioning process is not far-fetched. EDS, the large technology company, went through a similar visioning process in the 1990s.[3] In reaction to expectations about plateaued future growth, 150 EDS managers from across the country and around the world came to EDS headquarters, thirty at a time, to begin the visioning process. Their charge was to consider in detail the threats to the current economic engine of EDS. Each group or "wave" was given a "discovery assignment" to look at one segment of the industry. The wave participants involved their direct reports in this discovery process. An integration team then boiled the ideas of the waves down to produce a draft of a strategic vision. This draft was debated formally and informally throughout the company. In the end, more than two thousand people, devoting nearly thirty thousand person-hours, participated in the creation of the new vision. The resulting vision was broader, more encompassing, and more dynamic than one that a group of senior managers could have created. More important, the process engendered the commitment of all employees throughout the company. In fact, those who participated in the process thought that it had contributed as much to leadership development as it had to vision creation. Following this visioning process, the company initiated a series of joint ventures, experiments, and new products that would have been inconceivable just a few years before. EDS gained an important source of competitive advantage in developing leadership throughout its ranks.

This vision process looks very different from the normal, top-down orientation. Consider some of the advantages. First, it broadens the skill set of those involved. Instead of just thinking operationally about how to implement a vision, employees at all levels are expected to think strategically about the future direction of the organization. This process requires people to enlarge their knowledge base through talking with customers, analysts, and other employees about the current problems of the firm and its future. This puts them "in the know" and can help build a stronger sense of *competence.*

Second, because employees are not just involved operationally but also strategically, this process helps broaden their ability to influence the organization. Hence, employees feel more like players in the system rather than merely cogs that implement someone else's vision. This feeling can help build a stronger sense of *impact.*

Regarding the third advantage, consider this: What is more compelling to you, something that is given to you or something that you help create? Do you remember the first time you saved up for something as a child that you bought with your own money? Maybe it was a bike, a baseball glove, or a toy. Whatever it was, it was special because it came from your own hard work. And you probably took special care of it, too. When we have invested our own "sweat equity" in something, we are more likely to believe in it and to want to ensure its success. Similarly, a vision that people are part of creating is more likely to become a part of them. This kind of vision process increases the chances that that the vision will have *meaning,* and it enhances people's sense of *self-determination.*

Fourth, in addition to facilitating greater empowerment, this participative process is also likely to create a more comprehensive vision, one that takes into consideration multiple perspectives that would be lost if the CEO or top management team created the vision statement unilaterally. So not only do people feel more empowered as a result of the process, but the end result is likely to be a better product as well.

Finally, developing a compelling new vision implies deep change for an organization. Deep change often engenders resistance from employees. But when they are genuinely involved in the process, resistance is less likely to be a problem because employees have ownership of the resulting vision.

At this point, you may be thinking, "But however we got it, the vision is already in place." Keep in mind, however, that an effective vision is not static—especially in the rapidly changing environment in which most businesses are situated today. A good vision is revisited often and revised as needed to keep up with changing circumstances. A company doesn't have to be in dire straits to adopt the process that the CEO in our story used. In fact, the opposite is true: increasingly, successful organizations are those that are nimble in charting their future direction, even as they remain steadfast about their core values.

Consider the case of Roger Ackerman, who transformed Corning into one of the bright starts of the digital age. While keeping the Corning values of quality and innovation intact, he sold off the company's well-known cookware division and developed a strategic advantage in optical fiber. In four years, he increased Corning's market value from about $9 billion to around $50 billion.[4] So the challenge is to preserve the core values of the company while creating a dynamic vision that keeps the organization responsive to its environment.

 The opportunity to build empowerment through the process of creating a vision is one that every organization can take advantage of. Think about what kind of process you can use in your own organization to renew your vision statement. What can you do to ensure that your process for recreating your vision contributes to the goal of fashioning a climate of empowerment?

■ Vision as a Discipline

Creating an empowering vision is a discipline that takes courage, commitment, and persistence. To begin with, it is a natural tendency for the leader of a system to want to be in control. And it often is more comfortable for employees to believe that the leader is in control. They may feel safer and more secure believing that the leader knows with certainty the right path for the future. The process we have described runs counter to these tendencies. It requires leaders to admit that they don't have a crystal ball and that they do not know what the "right" vision is. In so doing, leaders make themselves vulnerable. They have to open themselves to listen to the voice of their people. They have to give up some control and accept that the end result probably won't be exactly what they would have envisioned unilaterally. What they gain, however, is likely to be a fuller and better vision and one, furthermore, that employees are more committed to.

Second, we all want quick results, but creating a vision through a participative process takes time. In the scenario we presented earlier, it took a couple of months for the envisioning team to formulate and revise the vision they ultimately presented to the CEO. There is a compensating gain, however: The overall time to implementation is likely to be shorter for two reasons. First, the buy-in phase will practically disappear, given that people already have buy-in due to their involvement at numerous steps in the process. Second, the implementation is likely to be quicker because of the high levels of empowerment and commitment that the process engenders. In the EDS example we described, the company developed several product and service initiatives that would have been otherwise inconceivable in such a short time.

Third, this process takes resources. It takes time away from people's normal assignments; in the case of our idealized scenario, the visioning process required thousands of person hours. It also required some travel to meet with customers and analysts. None of this is cheap, but if the vision truly works, the payoff can be huge. Because of its visioning process, EDS was able to embrace the digital age more quickly than its competitors, thus making them a leader today in e-business consulting.

Fourth, the process doesn't really end. Our scenario may have suggested that the process stops with the presentation of the vision to the CEO. But this is far from the truth. As we have indicated, an effective vision is dynamic. If we're going to live by a vision, it must be continually renewed and refreshed as conditions change. Depending on the velocity of change in your environment, the vision may need to be revisited in large or small ways annually, quarterly, or even more often. Though everyone should be charged with monitoring the environment, one way to accomplish periodic updating is to make a small team responsible for revisiting the vision on a regular basis and recommending when a full-scale *re-visioning* effort is needed. Like the company in our scenario, all employees must feel that the visioning processing begins and ends with them. Yes, giving the vision this kind of priority means significant work, but the alternative is a vision that guides no one because it has become hopelessly out of date.

CHAPTER SUMMARY

Vision provides direction to employees by aligning them to the future of the organization. A clear vision helps to keep people moving in the same direction even in the absence of direct supervision. This alone is consistent with empowered action.

But if our goal is to create a company of leaders, we need to pay attention to both the content of the organization's vision and the process whereby it is created. A vision becomes empowering when it fosters meaning, self-determination, competence, and impact. In terms of content, an empowering vision evokes passion, creates challenge, and makes a connection to a legacy. In terms of process, such a vision involves employees in creating or re-creating the vision so that they can take ownership of it.

Lest this account of vision seem one-sided, keep in mind that the discipline of vision operates in creative tension with another discipline of empowerment, security and support. We turn to this discipline next.

The Third Discipline

Continuous Support and Security

I n 1998 Durk Jager was brought in as chairman and CEO of Procter & Gamble, Co. His job was to transform the bureaucracy into a nimble giant able to compete in the hypercompetitive business environment. Jager did much of what we talked about in Chapter Four. He articulated a compelling vision of the future and set challenging stretch goals. He made people uncomfortable with the status quo. He pushed them in ways they had never been pushed before. But he also virtually broke the spirit of the organization and resigned under pressure from the board after only seventeen months on the job.[1] What happened?

As we discussed in Chapter Two, a system that fosters empowerment is one that manages competing tensions and keeps

opposing forces in a delicate balance. Among some other diffi-
culties, Jager failed this balancing act. He pushed the organization and its people to the extreme. Employees initially resisted.
Eventually they were paralyzed. This was a company with an
entrenched corporate culture and little history of radical change.
What Jager ignored was the need employees had for support
and security during periods of deep change.

The emphasis of this chapter is on the importance of recognizing the innate human need for security and support as you
attempt to nurture a climate of leadership amidst the chaos and
uncertainty that accompany significant change. Too much focus
on a new vision without a compensating focus on providing security and support leads to a system that feels out of control to
employees. Too much focus on security and support without the
energy that comes from a challenging vision leads to stagnation
and lethargy. A system that encourages empowerment is one
that brings together the energy of vision with a sense of support
and security. This requires managing the tensions inherent in
balancing these quadrants of the empowerment framework
(refer to Figure 2.1). If we want people to fly, it's not enough to
point the way to the sky. We also need to give them wings—and
a safety net that keeps them from a shattering fall.

*Take a few moments to respond to the following questions in your em-
powerment journal. Think about your own job. What gives you a sense
of comfort, a sense of security, a feeling of being supported and loved?
What happens to your ability to exercise leadership when these things
are absent in your work environment?*

We often take for granted the aspects of our environment
that provide us with a sense of security and support: a competent boss, close colleagues, fair policies and procedures, adequate training, and a sense of job security, to name a few. It is
only when they disappear that we realize how much our confi-

dence and performance depended on them. We get a new boss who is a tyrant, or a close colleague we considered a confidant leaves the organization for a new job, or rumors about downsizing leave us wondering whether we'll have a job next week. Suddenly our sense of security and support is violated, and we may question whether we're doing the right things or whether we even know what the right things are any more. Chances are, we'll hunker down and play it safe—and that means that our ability to exercise leadership is diminished.

A variety of elements help create the kind of secure and supportive work environment in which people can take chances and focus on creative ways of realizing the organization's vision. They include the following:

- A support network
- Resources to meet basic human needs
- Training to build skills and abilities
- A reward system that promotes initiative
- A culture in which mistakes are encouraged if they create learning

The discipline of safety and security consists of providing these elements as part of the organizational environment. Let's consider each in turn.

■ A Support Network

The most critical source of support and security is other human beings. The need for human contact is one of our most profound needs; babies who are denied close relationships and physical touch do not thrive and may even die. As adults, when we do not have a network of people we are comfortable with, whom we can confide in, who give us support, the result is anxiety and even paranoia. When we do have a supportive network of people, we feel a sense of safety and security that enables us to feel comfortable in taking initiative and trying new things. We can set our sights higher when we have a group of people behind us who support us regardless of how our initiative turns out.

Our support network at work might include our boss, coworkers, or team members, as well as people outside the organization, such as colleagues at other companies, close friends, and family members. It doesn't matter where the members of our support network are, just that we have people we can rely on for unconditional support.

What do these kinds of intensively supportive relationships look like in practice? An interesting example comes from the 2000 National Academy of Management Meetings in Toronto, Canada. Typically the presidential address is a dry affair that has little impact. The audience of thousands tolerates the speech because they want to see who wins the awards the organization gives out. In August 2000, the academy president, David Whetten, gave a very different kind of speech.[2] What is especially interesting is how his unusually powerful address came about.

The morning before he was to speak, David met with his two closest colleagues—friends he had known since graduate school—to share his speech with them and solicit their support. David's confidence in his friends' supportiveness allowed him to be comfortable in making himself vulnerable to their critique and feedback.

What happened next is everyone's worst nightmare. David's colleagues told him that his speech was just like every one before it—lifeless and dry. Although David had wanted their honest feedback, he was devastated by it. He had been working on this speech for months.

Here is where the friendship, the real support, kicked in. David's friends began asking him questions about the kind of speech that would have the impact that he wanted to achieve. David had answers. He knew what kinds of things he wanted to say. Sitting in the audience would be graduate students with low self-esteem who wondered whether they could ever finish their dissertations and get decent jobs. Also among the audience would be demoralized faculty who felt that they didn't have what it takes to be successful in the field. He wanted to help unleash the power within the audience by giving them hope, sharing how he overcame adversity as a new academic. Yet this would require a high degree of intimacy by sharing many of the setbacks he encountered in his personal and professional life. He wanted to demonstrate to the group that even the most hopeless situation can be turned around.

As David shared his thinking, his friends spent time discussing not only the content of the speech but also his state of mind. They wanted to make sure that he had the confidence necessary to give a high-impact speech.

The result was nothing less than phenomenal. Rather than basking in the glory of his position, he revealed his personal failures. In doing so he made it acceptable for people in the audience to consider and share their own feelings of inadequacy. He also provided a role model for what supportive relationships could look like. The audience was moved by David's remarks and gave him a standing ovation. Afterwards, the thousands of people who were there felt a special closeness to Dave, and many felt more personally empowered to be their best selves.

Communities of support like the one exemplified in this story are critical for people to feel a sense of safety and comfort amidst the chaos and uncertainty of change. They are an important coping mechanism. They allow people to trust and make themselves vulnerable so that learning and growth can take place. In today's business environment—with more people than ever working as temporary or contract employees, with people changing jobs more often across their careers, and with the traditional employment relationship becoming a thing of the past— these kinds of intense relationships are becoming more scarce, even as they are more needed.

Support Mechanisms

The importance of these networks is pretty obvious, but how can they be created and nurtured? First, for others to feel comfortable making themselves vulnerable to learn and grow, we must be first willing to make ourselves vulnerable. As David did, we might share one of our own failures or fears. This disclosure creates the common understanding necessary for intensive support. Consider, for example, the closeness that was created when a colleague of one of us admitted he was having a problem with depression. This disclosure allowed us to better understand his difficult situation, provide support by calling a contact at the Mayo Clinic for a referral, and take up the slack in his duties while he got the help he needed.

Second, we need to be present and available to each other. To provide support, people need to know that we are there for them regardless of schedules and deadlines. If they tell us, "This is something important," they'll know that we are willing to drop whatever we are doing to be present and available. Most often this "presence" will occur through a phone call or e-mail, but in times of crises it might mean traveling to wherever they are to be with them. When a junior colleague admitted having misgivings about his job during his first year of employment, this meant dropping our plans to prepare for our next day's teaching responsibilities so that we could sit down to listen to this person's woes and commiserate.

And third, real support requires us to be proactive. It's not just about waiting until others approach us in need. It means actively monitoring and checking in with those in our network to see how things are going. It means active listening so we can keep a pulse on those in our network. Continuing the example above of the junior colleague with misgivings, this meant stopping by this person's office each morning to ask, "How is it going?" and generally check in. Most days, the colleague's response was, "Fine," but some days, when the response seemed more lethargic, we made the time to close the door to find out more about how our colleague was doing.

Each of these courses of action requires initiative and perhaps even some sacrifice on our part. But the returns on these efforts become obvious when we need to draw on the support networks ourselves in times of need. Through our actions, we create a kind of bank account of goodwill that we can draw on as needed.

 Take a moment to reflect on your own support network. Who is in your network? What are you doing to nourish and grow your network? Also think about the quality of the support networks of the people in your unit or group. What can you do to help ensure that people have the networks they need? How do you invite them to be part of your network of support? How do you build community?

■ Resources to Meet Basic Human Needs

Psychologist Abraham Maslow became famous for his theory of motivation, which arranged human needs in a hierarchy, often depicted as a pyramid. Maslow argued that until human beings have their basic needs fulfilled, higher-order needs such as the needs for self-esteem or personal fulfillment do not become relevant. Among these basic needs is the need for security.

In the work environment, what this means is that it is difficult for employees to feel empowered to take initiative when they are worried about security and safety needs such as survival and well-being. Among the conditions that must be fulfilled in order for these needs to be met are personal safety, job security, and adequate staffing and financial resources.

Personal Safety

If employees are worried about their personal health and safety, it will be difficult for them to feel empowered. When we are concerned about our personal safety, our priority becomes protecting ourselves rather than opening ourselves up to be vulnerable and take initiative. Consequently, a work environment plagued by unclean working conditions, poor ventilation, inadequately maintained machinery, volatile coworkers or supervisors, harassment of any kind, or violence in the neighborhood works against a culture of empowerment.

Put yourself in the following situation:

One of us has a close friend, Tim, who works on a project with a volatile coworker. Tim is never sure of the coworker's mental state on any given day. On some days, the person is easy to get along with and receptive to suggestions and ideas. But on other days, the person is unpredictable—lashing out when suggestions are made and sulking when he doesn't get what he wants. Though the coworker has limited his tirades to verbal confrontations, Tim worries that physical manifestations may be around the corner. He cringes when he hears accounts of employee violence in the newspaper or on the TV, wondering whether these sorts of behaviors are in his coworker's future. The human resources department is aware of this person's problems and has talked to him about his behavior, but the company tolerates him because his work is brilliant.

Tim has learned to cope with the situation by avoiding the person whenever possible. He keeps his eyes open for the first opportunity to change jobs in the organization. He has given up on taking initiative and offering suggestions because he fears reprisals from his coworker. His approach is to "get along by going along." Because Tim fears for his personal safety, his sense of empowerment suffers. Particularly when it comes to self-determination, he feels that his ability to choose the appropriate course of action is severely restricted by the volatility of his coworker, a situation that creates a passive and obedient employee—hardly the "stuff" required for creating a company of leaders.

Job Security

Have you ever feared for your job? Upon realizing that your job was at risk, how did you respond? If you are like most people, your first reaction was to update your resume and begin looking for a new job. While you may have gone on fulfilling your basic duties, any initiative or innovation in your current job was probably put on hold until your job situation resolved itself.

Apart from the drain on energy and attention, employees will feel uncomfortable about taking any kind of risk when they are worried about their future with the organization. In particular, we have found in our own research on survivors of downsizing that employees will be hesitant to take initiative if they are worried that any improvements in productivity and efficiency that follow from empowerment will ultimately lead to layoffs.[3] This kind of "empowerment," which translates as "do more with less," is actually a disincentive for leadership behavior.

The idea of providing employment security in today's competitive world seems to be at odds with what most firms are doing. Yet there are notable exceptions. When General Motors opened its innovative Saturn division, it guaranteed people job security except in the most extreme circumstances. The feeling that making improvements would not lead to job displacement gave Saturn employees the freedom to find ways to become more productive and efficient. Similarly, Herb Kelleher, CEO of Southwest Airlines, says that employment security is one of the company's most important tools for building partnerships with employees. "Certainly there were times when we could have made substantially more profits in the short-term if we had furloughed people, but we didn't. . . . [W]e were looking at our employees' and our company's longer-term interests. . . [A]s it turns out, providing job security imposes additional discipline because if your goal is to avoid layoffs, then you hire very sparingly."[4]

Notice the word *discipline* in Kelleher's remarks about hiring. Committing to job security for employees may seem foolish unless it is paired with the necessary discipline to manage the size of the workforce, just as guaranteeing personal safety to employees means managing resources intelligently so that safety can be a priority. Like everything else of value, the benefits of empowerment come at a price.

Adequate Staffing and Financial Resources

One *Fortune* 100 company we have worked with operates with a very lean workforce. Company leaders boast about how they have grown the business without increasing their workforce or their budgets; people are doing more with less. Although that is true, employees at this firm will tell you that they are being run ragged. They can barely keep their heads above the water. Their work is suffering and as a result so are their personal lives. No one feels very empowered to take initiative; they don't have the energy to do so.

Clearly, there is a fine line between operating lean and being anorexic. Is manpower so tight in your organization that people are working extreme hours and feeling overloaded? If so, it's likely that employees don't feel empowered to take initiative. They are simply doing all they can just to survive in a reactive mode. They will not have the time and energy required to think about new ideas, let alone act on them. Moreover, if budgets are so tight that even tasks such as preventive maintenance are being neglected, people will soon discover that it's pointless to suggest initiatives that won't get funding. Efficiency is important, but every organization also needs some slack in the system so that time and resources are available for reflection, initiative, and experimentation.

3M, the highly successful maker of adhesives and disks, has a policy that encourages employees to spend 15 percent of their time on ideas that might result in new products. This focus on innovation is an important part of their corporate culture. Though employees are expected to work hard, they also are given the release time necessary to be reflective and think in innovative and creative ways. This is how they ensure that the majority of their revenues are generated from products that are less than five years old.

Think about the resources you have access to in your organization. Does your workload allow you the time and energy necessary for reflection and initiative? Do you have the resources necessary for empowerment? What can you do to help your people become proactive rather than reactive?

■ Training to Build Skills and Abilities

Whereas providing adequate resources creates a platform for empowered behavior, developing the crucial dimension of competence requires that people have the opportunity to grow their skills and competencies. Training is thus an essential component of a system that fosters empowerment—that is, a system that relies on the skill and initiative of employees at all levels of the organization to identify and resolve problems, initiate changes in work methods, and take responsibility for quality.

Providing for continual skill development has an additional benefit: It helps build employees' sense of employment security because they know they are being trained for the needs of the future whether they continue in the organization or eventually need to find work elsewhere. General Electric has made this kind of "employability" a key part of its business strategy.

Beyond training in the technical skills needed to do their jobs, employees need additional types of training in order to be empowered and operate in self-managed ways. Training in basic finance, for example, can help employees understand how to make good business decisions. For this reason, instruction in finance for non-finance people can be a particularly valuable educational offering. Training in people skills, time management, creative problem solving, and stress reduction are relevant to nearly everyone. Often organizations seeking empowerment create some kind of team structure. Working in teams involves a distinct set of competencies that require training, such as team building, conflict management, decision making through consensus, and management of diversity.

Whatever skills employees feel they need to be self-managing should be given priority. The hallmark of Arthur Andersen is the opportunity its people have to build a portfolio of professional skills and equity in a career that takes them to the top of their field, whether they stay and practice as a long-term member of the firm or as an alumnus. Arthur Andersen, the large accounting firm, consistently spends more time and money providing development opportunities for its people than any other organization. It offers 135 hours of training per employee per year—the equivalent of more than three weeks of work time in educational opportunities. Through this intensive training, Arthur Andersen gives employees the capability for real initiative and leadership.[5] One employee acknowledged, "You can learn more in one year here than in several years in most organizations."[6]

 Take an inventory of the training currently being provided in your organization or unit. Does this training provide the kinds of capabilities that are needed for people to display initiative and other leadership behaviors? Do you understand the educational desires of your people?

■ A Reward System That Promotes Initiative

Providing a living wage fulfills the fundamental need for basic survival. Beyond that, a competitive base salary contributes to employees' sense of security and demonstrates that the organization values them. A base salary, however, has limited power to encourage leadership behavior, since it is given regardless of how well the company does and has little relationship to how much employees take initiative, come up with creative solutions to business problems, go the extra mile to respond to customers' needs, or make changes that have significant impact on the organization's performance. In short, a base salary is essentially disconnected from empowered behavior. Yet we all know that we must reward the behavior we want to see. If we want employees to act as owners of the business, the reward system needs to reflect this value.

Compensation, of course, is a huge subject, worthy of a book in itself. Here we want to focus on using rewards as one element among many in a system that fosters empowerment. In general, there are two kinds of rewards that can be aligned with the goal of encouraging empowerment: paying for organizational performance and paying for individual performance.

Paying for Organizational Performance

A number of companies have instituted systems that reward employees for gains in organizational performance. One of the most common is the provision of stock options, whereby employees are given the option to buy stock in the company at a future time at its current price or some set price. The idea is that the employee will benefit when the stock price increases in value.

Stock options were once reserved for those at the top levels of the firm, but today many firms, particularly small start-ups, are offering them to employees at every level of the organization. Even the baristas at Starbucks and the burger-flippers at Wendy's get stock options these days. In large organizations, unfortunately, this kind of reward system often seems too far removed from the specific efforts of an individual employee. Often employees feel that too many factors affect stock price, such as industry forces and general economic conditions, for their individual behavior to make much of a difference. Nevertheless, stock options do send a message that employees have a direct stake in the organization's performance.

In the mid 1990s, Siebel Systems, Inc., a developer of customer-support software based in San Mateo, California, implemented a companywide stock option program. Siebel generated sales of $77 million in the first nine months of 1997, up from just $8 million for all of 1995. In 1996 the company's head count tripled, and it doubled again in the first nine months of 1997. Ask Siebel employees how the stock option program impacted them and they will tell you it made them feel and act as owners of the firm. They took action as they saw fit, knowing they would benefit from any company gains.[7]

Another type of reward that pays individuals based on the performance of the organization is profit sharing. Typically this type of reward is linked to the performance of a unit or plant. Consequently, employees feel that the reward, more so than stock options, is connected to outcomes on which they can have some direct impact. And it reinforces the idea that worthwhile actions and initiatives are those that have a measurable impact on the company's performance. The effect is to broaden the horizons of employees by encouraging them to think about how they can have an impact on the collective good of the organization.

Paying for Individual Performance

Paying for organizational performance facilitates leadership behavior by encouraging people to think like owners of the business, but the connection to individual performance may not be strong. Accordingly, a complementary approach is to reward individuals for displaying empowered behavior.

Of course, there is nothing new in the idea of providing rewards for individual performance, such as bonuses and merit pay. In terms of fostering a climate of empowerment, the key is to identify the kinds of leadership behaviors the company wants to encourage, publicize them, and create a clear line of sight between these desired aspects of performance and individual rewards. In short, both the company and the employees need to be very clear about what kinds of actions are valued. Reward conformity and compliance, and that is what you are likely to get. If you want empowered action, individual rewards need to be tied to demonstrations of leadership, such as initiative, risk taking, and innovation that have a genuine impact on the organization.

In the case of merit pay, for example, employees' leadership accomplishments might be evaluated annually, ideally by using a 360-degree system that takes into consideration the assessments of subordinates, peers, superiors, and even customers. Innovation and initiative can also be rewarded through suggestion systems and other ways of paying individual employees for ideas that save money or improve quality. The key is to demonstrate that employees will directly benefit from initiatives, ideas, and actions that materially benefit the organization.

Although we have focused on the issue of pay, keep in mind that there are other kinds of rewards as well. One of the most important is recognition. This might be a pat on the back for a job well done, a mention at a staff meeting or in the company newsletter, or a plaque in a public place. Publicly acknowledging the achievements of people who exhibit empowered behavior reinforces the message being given by aligning extrinsic rewards with desired behavior.

One word of warning about emphasizing pay for individual performance: This kind of emphasis can create competition among employees, particularly if some kind of rank ordering is used to determine the amount of the reward. As a result, overemphasizing this type of reward can discourage effective collaboration and teamwork. The solution is to include collaboration as one of the aspects of performance that is being rewarded, and to couple pay for individual performance with some pay for organizational or group performance.

Lincoln Electric, a world leader in welding and cutting products, is famous for its system of pay for individual performance based on piece-rate (a kind of manufacturing-production commission). Employees are rewarded for each piece of quality product that they create. The downside of most piece-rate systems is intense and often counterproductive competition among employees who refuse to help each other or share ideas. To ensure that employees work cooperatively with each other and share ideas on how to boost productivity, their annual bonus (which amounts to tens of thousands of dollars from the company's profit-sharing program) is based on how cooperative and willing to share ideas they are. The company also guarantees employment after three years of service. Through this well-defined group of incentives, Lincoln encourages and compensates individual initiative and responsibility. Employees work together to reduce costs and improve quality. These individual and cooperative efforts create a more profitable company, the success of which each person shares according to his or her own contribution.

Think about the formal and informal reward systems in your company. What kinds of actions are being rewarded? What kinds of actions are discouraged either explicitly or implicitly? What kinds of reward system would help create a company of leaders?

■ A Culture in Which Mistakes Are Encouraged If They Create Learning

Imagine the following scenario. You are the president of a very large and successful company. In one of his first assignments as a senior manager, one of your people makes a poor decision that costs the firm somewhere in the area of $1 million. You call the person into your office, and immediately he begins apologizing profusely and saying he deserves to be fired. How do you respond?

This very incident happened to James Burke, who later became the CEO of Johnson & Johnson—only he was the one doing the apologizing. The story has become legendary in the company. When Burke said that he deserved to be fired, the president retorted, "What do you mean fire you—I just spent more than $1 million on your education through this mishap!"

This tale gets told and retold because of the message it delivers to people at Johnson & Johnson: "We expect you to take risks. We expect that sometimes you will fail. When you do fail, our aim is not to punish you, but to help you learn from your mistake." What the story says is that this message is more than just comforting words; it is a lived reality.

The point should be clear: It is futile to tell employees that they should act in empowered ways and then punish them when they take risks. It isn't that the mistake should be overlooked or blithely dismissed, but rather that the emphasis should be on what can be learned from it, what might be done next time to get a better result. It's fair to hold people accountable for learning from their mistakes, but when accountability means never making a mistake in the first place, people aren't likely to risk doing anything truly innovative. Instead they will protect themselves by following orders and asking permission before taking action.

To be a leader is to be constantly learning and growing. If we want people to act as leaders, we need to acknowledge that there will be a learning curve and consequently that there will be some failures along the way. Someone who never fails probably isn't stretching enough.

In our need to feel in control as managers, it's all too easy to demand perfection from those around us. Truly implementing the idea that mistakes are to be expected, and indeed can be valuable learning opportunities, requires that all our people at all levels send this message in their behavior as well as their words. This is a part of the courage that creating a climate of empowerment requires of us.

Think about your organization's culture. Think about the last time you witnessed a mistake being punished. What impact did that have? How could the mistake have been handled differently to encourage learning?

■ Security and Support as a Discipline

Creating the sense of community that comes with the discipline of security and support requires continuous attention. It means we constantly monitor the pulse of the human side of the system to ensure that employees have the requisite security and support. One monitor might be a monthly employee survey from a stratum of the population to find out what the issues are that are on people's minds. It might be "management by walking around"—spending time walking by people's workplaces, touching base with them about the issues at hand. It might come from regularly eating in the employee cafeteria with different groups of people to gauge their perspectives. However it is done, empowering leaders stay in touch with the feelings of their people.

We've talked about Herb Kelleher of Southwest Airlines before—he is a master at monitoring the pulse of his organization. It is not unusual to see him visiting with the night shift of machinists or baggage handlers. This occurs without any pre-announcement. At least once a month, he joins his employees on a flight, serving peanuts and checking seat assignments as though he were a flight attendant. He asks employees how they are doing and listens to their answers. Not only does this help him stay in touch with his people, he also gets to interact with his customers.

The discipline of security and support also requires a long-term view. Employment security, training, reward systems, and organizational culture require real investments in people—investments that take time to pay off. Only when these investments unleash the power in your workforce do they pay handsome returns. So this discipline requires some real courage on the part of the leader to not acquiesce to the intense pressure for short-term results created by stockholders. This is one reason it is sometimes easier for private companies to create the intensive support we have emphasized in this chapter.

In the same vein, it may be easier to create this discipline of security and support in smaller organizations. In smaller firms, it is easier for leaders to keep track of their organization's pulse and create real community. This is why some organizations continually spin off new divisions and units as their numbers increase: to maintain the smallness that helps preserve and maintain community. For example, W. L. Gore and Associates, Inc., the maker of high-tech polymers, discourages any hierarchy by allowing any unit to grow to no more than a hundred employees. This ensures that the team-based environment and direct person-to-person relationships exist among all Gore associates.

Creating an environment of support and security takes real work and commitment—in a word, *discipline*—but this discipline is essential for getting the payoffs that come from creating a company of leaders.

CHAPTER SUMMARY

In this chapter, we have explored the importance of balancing the change orientation of vision and challenge with the discipline of providing adequate security and support. We considered several elements of the organizational environment that can create this essential requirement of empowered action: a support network, resources to meet basic needs, training to build skills and abilities, a reward system that promotes initiative, and a culture that encourages mistakes as long as they create learning.

Providing for these conditions sends a strong message of caring for employees' well-being, which is worthwhile in itself as a way of encouraging employees to feel connected to the organization and committed to its success. More important for our purposes, however, attending to safety and security needs is a necessary complement to challenging people to grow, innovate, and take initiative. Too often we see challenging others and nurturing them as an either-or choice. The truth is that empowering management does both.

The Fourth Discipline
Continuous Openness and Trust

In the last two chapters, we have focused on promoting leadership behavior by managing the competing tensions of vision/challenge and security/support. In this chapter and the next we address the second set of competing tensions illustrated in Figure 2.1—that between creating a climate of openness and trust while maintaining sufficient structure to provide necessary guidance. This tension centers on the issue of control. On the one hand, creating openness and trust means *giving up* control in order to share it with subordinates; on the other hand, managers must *maintain* a suitable degree of control to provide adequate guidance and structure. As we will see, both giving up and maintaining control are necessary to encourage empowered action.

■ Openness and Trust in an Empowering Environment

In our research, we have found that two of the biggest barriers to workplace empowerment are (1) leaders who are not open to sharing business information with employees, and (2) leaders who centralize decision making at high levels of the organizational hierarchy, not trusting that employees can or will act in the interests of the firm. The business press is replete of stories of leaders who hoard sensitive information that would aid employees in taking initiative. All too often, in the wake of a downsizing or bankruptcy, employees lament that if only they had known things were so bad, they would have done things differently. If only they had known more about the financial health of the organization, they say they would have offered up real ideas on cost savings or innovation. Similarly, the business press provides countless tales of dictatorial bosses who demand complete control and squelch any initiative on the part of employees. To create the company of leaders this book is all about, leadership must encourage the open flow of information and mutual trust. In this chapter we focus on how you can develop this fourth discipline of openness and trust to unleash the power bottled up within your workforce.

Openness

Openness is about creating a transparent organization. A transparent organization has no secrets. In a transparent organization, even sensitive information is shared with employees at all levels of the organization with the understanding that the information will be used with discretion. Employees are privy to the profit-and-loss statements that often remain in the hands of senior management. In an organization that is open, employees have knowledge of strategic moves being undertaken by the organization so they can be sure that their own actions and behaviors are appropriately aligned. Rather than being uptight about the potential for informational leakage, an environment that values this kind of openness worries more about what happens when employees are not "in the know."

To make good decisions, people need to have access to relevant information about the business environment and the performance of the organization: profits, customer satisfaction, scrap, budgets, market share, productivity, defects, warranty information, and so on. Such information even includes privileged information—sensitive, guarded information that is not publicly available. Openness means, in short, treating employees as partners in running the company. Withholding information on financial performance, strategy, and operations delivers the message that people can't be trusted—that they are too dumb to understand the information or that they will misuse it. But you cannot ask for leadership from people if you keep secrets from them.

What does this kind of openness look like in practice? Opening the books to employees and sharing sensitive information about the company's market share and growth opportunities, as well as about competitors' strategies, is a step in the right direction. Frito-Lay, for instance, has computerized its entire product development system so that everyone in the organization has information about the sales volumes across product lines. The Honda plant in Marysville, Ohio, has a large scoreboard that gives ongoing detailed information about the plant's performance.

Whole Foods, a chain of natural foods grocery stores, goes even farther. The chain is growing by leaps and bounds; between 1991 and 1996, it enjoyed sales growth of 864 percent and net income growth of 438 percent as it expanded from ten to sixty-eight stores.[1] Whole Foods shares detailed financial and performance information with every employee, including individual salaries. Every Whole Foods store has a book that lists the previous year's salary and bonus of all 6,500 employees. In addition to conveying a powerful message that employees can be trusted, this open disclosure requires that the organization make a special effort to keep salaries fair internally and externally.

Ideally, the kind of openness we are talking about is characterized by *open-book management*. Created by Jack Stack of Springfield ReManufacturing Corporation, open-book management requires that employees have access to all the numbers, from the company's income and cash-flow statements to the balance sheet. Stack knew if the plant he worked for was to succeed, all employees not only had to do their best but also had to contribute all their wisdom and ideas for enhancing the plant's performance. And this required real knowledge about the business, even to the point of sharing this kind of sensitive financial information. The ultimate result for Springfield ReManufacturing is having "700 internal auditors in every function of the company."[2]

Of course, just throwing information at people is not enough. Even motivated people cannot contribute to enhancing organizational performance if they can't understand or use the information that is shared with them. People need to be trained how to read, interpret, and use the information that is provided. At Stack's company, blue-collar workers and even secretaries had the equivalent of a college business education. The company has provided in-house business education in financial management and marketing. When Johnsonville Foods, the Wisconsin-based sausage maker, adopted self-managing teams that took over all elements of team management from product development to hiring and firing team members, the company brought in a professor from a local community college to teach employees basic financial analysis so that they could read and understand financial statements.[3]

When employees have live, hot information—not sales last quarter but sales right now—they can adjust on the fly. This profoundly changes the way decisions can be made in a firm by driving significant decision making far down into the organization. For example, real-time information lets Cisco devolve power radically.[4] Every supervisor at any level in the organization can see everything about the operation he or she runs. At any time in the quarter, first-line managers can look at margins and products and know exactly what the effect of their decisions will be. They can act faster and more intelligently—and top management is more comfortable with letting them act.

We have dwelled in some detail on openness because it is a foundation for the other ways of sharing control with employees. It's meaningless to ask people to be more involved in improving the business through initiative and innovation—to act like leaders—unless they have the information they need to make meaningful and competent decisions. Confining information to a privileged group amounts to saying that only those in the group are entrusted with exercising leadership. For this reason, the extent of openness by a company's leaders is a good index of an organization's commitment to creating a climate of empowerment.

Mutual Trust

Asking people to act like leaders also involves a significant degree of trust on everyone's part. Trust means several things. First, trust is a belief that other people can be counted on to do what they say they will do. In this sense, we trust others when they are reliable. Second, trust means having faith in other people's honesty, that they say what they mean and mean what they say. Third, trust means believing in other people's good faith. When people trust each other, they assume that neither person will take advantage of the other.[5]

All these meanings of trust are relevant to empowerment. Mutual trust acts as a lubricant in a system that fosters empowerment. Managers feel more comfortable giving up some control to allow subordinates freedom to take initiative when they can trust that their subordinates will act responsibly, reliably, and competently, and that they will be honest about what they have done and what the consequences have been. For their part, subordinates feel more comfortable behaving in empowered ways when they can trust that managers mean what they say and genuinely want them to show initiative and take risks. Subordinates need to believe that they will not be punished for the inevitable mistakes or that their freedom of action will not be circumscribed or withdrawn the moment they exercise it. Trust is fragile; it can be violated by a single act of malfeasance. And once it has been violated, it takes a long time to restore, if indeed it can be restored at all.

How can this kind of mutual trust be developed? Typically trust builds through a history of interaction that indicates reliability, honesty, and good faith. It can be kick-started with a single act of vulnerability by one party in the relationship. If I make myself vulnerable to you, even when you have a chance to take advantage of my vulnerability, I begin the process of building mutual trust.

Sound irrational—even foolish? Consider the example of Gene Cattabiani as related in a story of his first days as a general manager at Westinghouse Corporation.[6]

The company had a history of extreme distrust between union and management. In particular, it had a very adversarial relationship with one union. Gene was new to the job and had no history with the union. In one of his first days on the job, the union struck, and ten thousand people walked off the job. As Gene prepared for his first negotiation with the union, his senior managers counseled him on how to handle the situation. They told him that there were two issues that were so sensitive that he must never discuss them with the union: plants in the South and outsourcing. Plants in the South were located in right-to-work states and were not unionized. Outsourcing was a threat to the job security and growth of the unionized workforce.

What did Gene do with this advice? He began his initial meeting with the union by saying the following: "You certainly made your point clear this morning when you walked off the job. As the new general manager I would very much like to turn over a new leaf and start afresh with you. To get us started, today there are only two things that I hope we can spend our time on: (1) plants in the South and (2) outsourcing."

As you might imagine, both the company executives and the union officials were speechless. Gene was bringing up the most sacred issues, the issues that were never to be talked about. Was he crazy or did he understand something that is seldom understood in organizations?

The following quotation by Michael Thompson explains why Gene's actions were so powerful in building trust:

> If you wish to exert an influence, you must be open to being influenced. That is a law of our human interactions, as true in dealing with coworkers and political constituents as it is in the relationship with your own children. To truly influence others—as distinct from the use of raw power, coercion, or bribe—requires an openness to the influence of the other. Vulnerability is one word for that kind of openness. But it's a dirty word to most of us, isn't it? It implies a certain weakness, a susceptibility to something harmful or negative; indeed, we associate it with victimization. Our meaning here, of course, is quite the contrary. Mature vulnerability assumes the existence of a strong and well-developed ego that makes victimization by others unlikely. . . . [W]e have a strong sense of our identity, yet we must be able when appropriate to set it aside in service of the larger goal of truly relating to others. This simultaneous sense of both self and selflessness, so enigmatic to others, is the natural possession of those with a mature spiritual life.[7]

Gene Cattabiani was making himself vulnerable. He was taking the first steps in building trust. Of course, he was taking a risk. The union could have responded by taking advantage of his efforts to create an open and trusting climate. In fact, Gene's act of making himself vulnerable went a long way in breaking rampant distrust and building a more trusting relationship. He was able to work with the union to create a more collaborative environment that encouraged employees to produce better products and provide superior customer service.

This kind of trust is very difficult to build, but it is critical to creating the kind of environment where people feel comfortable about sharing control. In the case of managers who want to encourage empowerment on the part of their subordinates, it is clearly the manager who needs to take that first step of making oneself vulnerable. It is the manager who operates from a presumed position of control and authority, and who therefore has something to give.

Yet through the very act of making himself vulnerable, Gene was providing a model of the kind of behavior he hoped for from his employees. Empowered behavior requires that employees make themselves vulnerable. Employees risk failure when taking initiative. Their ideas may bomb. It is often easier for employees to just do what they are told—to be obedient and compliant. Gene was modeling the kinds of vulnerability that undergird trust and that are so critical for empowered behavior.

If openness and mutual trust are necessary in an empowering climate, why are they so rare in corporate life? Clearly, one answer is that they seem to be the opposite of control, and giving up control does not come easily for most of us. Many large organizations developed under the tutelage of a command-and-control bureaucracy. In this kind of system, managers give the orders and the rest of the organization obeys. A command-and-control organization creates structures, processes, and systems aimed at reducing variation and risk. In such a system, managers and subordinates alike have been conditioned to believe that control must be hoarded rather than shared.

It should be clear that this approach is the opposite of cultivating trust in people to do the right thing and their trust in managers to let them do it. Yet learning to share control can be one of the most difficult transitions a manager makes. The next section explores why this is so.

■ The Threat Inherent in Giving Up Control

In our work with executives, we often run the exercise shown in Worksheet 6.1. Put yourself in the shoes of the manager as you read and rate yourself on each scenario.

If you are like most of the executives we work with, you have rated yourself fairly highly in terms of empowerment in each of these scenarios. Moreover, the response of the executives we have worked with is generally positive:

- "This person is doing the right thing even when it is difficult to do."
- "This person has courage and takes necessary risks for the good of the business."
- "The manager challenged the status quo."

We also ask executives to repeat the exercise, this time with a different scale: indicating how comfortable they would be if each story was a description of the behavior of one of their direct reports.

 Take a moment to do this yourself. On a scale from one to ten, with ten being most empowered, rate each scenario in terms of your comfort level with having one of your direct reports operating in this way.

If you are like most of the executives who have taken this exercise, you have expressed some reservations about your

■ Worksheet 6.1. Giving Up Control Assessment ■

In your empowerment journal, on a scale from one to ten (with ten being very empowered), rate the extent to which you believe you are acting in empowered ways.

_____**Scenario 1**

As a middle manager, you have come up with a new system for working with remote locations. The system is a threat to what is currently a highly centralized operation. Careful analysis has shown that the change would result in lower cost, increased quality, and better coordination. Furthermore you feel intuitively that the change is "right." In making this initial proposal, you have received discouraging responses from those above and below. You nevertheless have made a long-term commitment to gradually sell your idea.

_____**Scenario 2**

As a newly assigned middle manager attending your first meeting with your new group, you listen to a proposal made by your boss. Given your considerable experience with a similar subject at your previous location, you are quite knowledgeable about the proposal's shortcomings. You therefore offer a blunt but constructive assessment of the drawbacks in the boss's proposal.

_____**Scenario 3**

A CEO, known to sometimes act as a tyrant, has decided that the activities in a certain function should be expanded. The analytic task has fallen to you, a middle manager, five layers down in the hierarchy. You eventually conclude that the function should be eliminated. Your immediate superior tells you to "redo" the analysis. After much soul searching, you turn in the report recommending the elimination. Your superiors then decide that you should make the presentation directly to the CEO. You agree to do so.

_____**Scenario 4**

Some years ago as plant manager, you were told that a new product must be launched. The survival of the corporation was dependent upon its success. After you analyzed the situation, you concluded that the only way the project could be accomplished was to make some significant promises to the local union. The promises potentially had companywide implications and were unlikely to be approved by corporate human resources. You decided to give the union what they were asking for, and you proceeded.

subordinates acting in such empowered ways. People tend to voice concerns such as these:

- "This person would be going too far in taking these actions."
- "I would worry that this person is taking risks that are too big."
- "This person is going beyond her zone of authority."

Why do you think we are often ambivalent about the empowerment of the people who work for us? When thinking in the abstract or about ourselves, most of us are quite comfortable with notions of initiative, risk, personal growth, and trust. We become much less comfortable, however, in thinking about these same characteristics when considering how we manage our own direct reports. We wonder about how much autonomy our people can handle without becoming loose cannons. We worry about losing control. We feel threatened.

Certainly there are reasons for this feeling of threat. Ceding authority to employees to make empowered decisions creates some risk for managers. Subordinates may behave in a way that serves their own interests when their own needs conflict with the collective interests of the organization. And even when they have the best of intentions, they may be incompetent or ignorant and make bad decisions.

But our difficulty in giving up control goes beyond worries about self-interested or inept subordinates. It is grounded in our learned identity as managers. When we measure our value by the authority we wield, as is often the case for managers and executives, we may feel threatened by employee empowerment. We may see subordinates as invading our turf and diluting our authority.

Research by Jeffrey Pfeffer indicates that this ambivalence on the part of those in authority is often a reason empowerment efforts fail. In an experiment, he had managers rate the financial results of a decision made by themselves and the financial results of a virtually identical decision made by subordinates. *Even in cases where the results of subordinate decisions were equal to and even better than the results of their own decision making, managers tended to rate their own decisions most favorably.*[8]

As human beings, we seem programmed to see ourselves in a favorable light. This positive bias helps keep us mentally healthy. If we are convinced that only we can do a given job best, it becomes illogical to share control with subordinates by letting them make significant decisions. Moreover, giving up control can be an affront to our often sensitive egos. Giving decision making authority to lower-level employees can signal to us that we are not so necessary, that we don't have the magic bullet to solve the organization's problems, and that we are dependent on the creativity and problem-solving skills of our people to perform successfully. Of course, all these things are true, but as managers and executives, we want to believe we have something special to bring to the table. After all, if our subordinates have these special qualities, why don't they have our jobs?

Apart from protecting our egos, it makes us feel good to take on responsibility to save other people worry and anxiety, and we're often rewarded for doing so. Yet in the process we don't see that others are capable of doing the same thing. Responsibility for decisions in organizations thus tends to migrate to higher levels than is necessary or optimal. Charles Handy notes that the Catholic Church has a word for this tendency: *subsidiarity.* A papal encyclical explained that this means "an injustice, a grave evil and a disturbance of right order for a larger and higher organization to arrogate to itself functions which can be performed efficiently by smaller and lower bodies."[9] We mean well when we take on problems and decisions that others could handle if we let them, but in doing so we are encouraging others to be dependent on us. That might be nice for our self-esteem, but it discourages leadership on the part of others.

What aspects of your authority can you envision willingly sharing with others? What kinds of decisions and initiatives do you feel you must reserve to yourself? Why is that so? Can you honestly say that you are the only person who can take on those decisions? If the issue is knowledge, experience, or training, can you envision working to give subordinates the chance to develop similar assets so that they can bring their creativity to bear on the decisions you now reserve for yourself?

The upshot of the inherent threat involved in giving up control is that many of us implicitly discourage empowerment by reinforcing control systems that, intentionally or unintentionally, send the message that we really do not trust people to exercise leadership. We create policy manuals that specify the various sorts of approvals employees must seek in decision making. We design reward systems that punish mistakes and discourage employee initiative. These kinds of control systems create pressures for conformity rather than encourage initiative and risk taking. When this happens, employees are apt to believe that an empowerment program is merely a guise to have them take on greater responsibility and assume more risks without additional rewards, accompanied by an increased chance of being blamed when thing go wrong.

Of course, as we will discuss in the next chapter, the right kind of control mechanisms are necessary to keep empowerment within bounds. The challenge thus becomes how to create an environment where we feel comfortable giving up control and involving people as partners in the organization. The next section considers specific ways of sharing control in an environment characterized by openness and trust. Keep in mind, however, that part of the answer is that empowerment doesn't mean giving up all control; we're talking about a company of leaders, not a company of unguided missiles. We discuss that half of the equation in the next chapter.

■ Ways of Sharing Control

Control means power—power to make decisions, power to allocate resources, power to tell others what to do and when to do it. Encouraging empowerment doesn't mean simply delegating this power, but rather sharing it responsibly and trusting others to do their part. Here we consider three ways that organizations and managers can share control and power: suggestion systems, job involvement, and high involvement.[10]

Suggestion Systems

Probably the oldest approach to sharing control is instituting a suggestion system whereby employees are asked to problem solve and produce ideas that will influence how the organization operates. Often employees are rewarded for good ideas that get implemented.

We're not talking about a suggestion box on the receptionist's desk, but about a systematic routine of soliciting ideas that tackle substantive business problems. Total quality management philosophies emphasize the importance of this kind of employee involvement. Quality circles involve groups of employees, often volunteers, who meet periodically to discuss ideas for improvements. Sometimes individual suggestion systems allow employees to share in the benefits of their ideas. For example, if an employee makes a suggestion that results in a cost savings of $10,000, the company might share some of the cost saving by giving back to the employee a certain percentage of the savings. This kind of reward provides an important incentive for employees to make suggestions.

Clearly, the value of this kind of suggestion system depends in part on the openness and trust we have just described; people will be better able to make powerful suggestions if they are well-informed and where there is mutual trust. A caveat, however: Although a suggestion system is an improvement over a traditional command-and-control bureaucracy in terms of empowerment, it moves only a small amount of control to lower-level employees, thus allowing managers to retain most, if not all, of their power. After all, in a suggestion system, managers still decide which ideas get implemented.

Job Involvement

Job involvement is an approach that focuses on giving employees more of a say in how they do their own work. Employees decide how and when the work is done. They have discretion to handle problems regarding their own job as they see fit. For example, when a customer calls in with a problem, rather than having to get approval from a supervisor for a course of action or look up the approved response in a procedures manual, the employee determines the best response for that customer. This kind of involvement focuses very explicitly on giving employees the self-determination so important for empowerment.

Often job involvement systems involve the use of work teams that manage themselves in terms of hiring, firing, disciplining, and scheduling. Aid Association for Lutherans (AAL), a mutual benefit association, moved to this kind of team structure in the early 1990s. Teams of employees determine their schedules so that they can offer extended hours of customer service. Team members cover for each other when on vacation or absent. And they are able to offer customers one-stop service and problem solving on the spot. No longer do they need to seek manager approval for a course of action—they can go ahead and give customers an immediate response. You can imagine what this kind of involvement has done for customer satisfaction.

With this kind of job involvement, managers transition from directing subordinates to teaching and coaching. Managers are no longer needed for approvals and oversight. Instead, they help employees develop the capabilities necessary to make good decisions. And without the worry of a manager looking over their shoulder and second-guessing their decisions, employees feel more comfortable taking initiative. Of course, sometimes managers have a hard time with this transition to teacher and coach because they feel that their power is being taken away. So they, too, need some training on how to develop their capability as a teacher and coach. AAL provided training like this for their managers. Most important, they gave the managers new strategic responsibilities (such as investigating new product offerings) that made them feel valued but also made it physically impossible to monitor employees as they had done in the past *and* still take care of their new responsibilities.

Job involvement goes a long way in giving employees the discretion to take initiative and act in empowered ways, but it, too, has limits. The high-involvement approach described next provides the ultimate release of power in your workforce.

High Involvement

The high-involvement approach takes empowerment yet another step. Also called a high-commitment approach, high involvement means that employees at all levels of the organization not only have control over their own work but also are invited to play a role in decisions concerning the organization's strategic direction. The high-involvement approach moves power, information, knowledge, and rewards to the lowest organizational level. This approach is based on the premise that individuals need to know about the organization, should be able to influence it, and should be rewarded for performance in order to care about organizational success. People in a high-involvement organization have the power to decide not only how to do their own work but also to influence the larger workings of their unit and even the entire organization.

To see how this works in practice, return for a moment to the Springfield ReManufacturing and Johnsonville Foods examples introduced earlier in the chapter. When General Motors canceled an order that represented 40 percent of Springfield's business, the firm averted a possible layoff by providing its people with information on what had happened and then letting them figure out how to grow the company and achieve the productivity improvements that would obviate layoffs. Rather than viewing this action as an attempt by top managers to put their burdens on lower-level employees, employees viewed it as an opportunity to be real partners with the organization. With the ingenuity of all employees, the organization was able to recover from the loss of business.[11]

Similarly at Johnsonville Foods, when the time came to make an important strategic decision about whether to take over a competitor's line of business, employees were able to make the appropriate decision because they knew how to run the numbers.[12] Though their CEO Ralph Stayer was reluctant to take on the new business because he did not believe they had sufficient manpower, the employees made the decision to accept the business, committing to working overtime for a year to ensure they would make it work. And the employees were right: They were able to take on the business successfully and integrate it into their organization.

In a high-involvement system, employees are real partners in the business decisions of the organization. As illustrated in the example of an empowering vision in Chapter Four, employees in a high-involvement system have a say in the strategic planning process and resulting goals for the organization. In this case, the visioning process was stimulated and a vision developed by a cross-sectional group of middle managers with the input of employees around the corporation. Although the CEO was supportive of the process, he stayed out of the visioning process (with the exception of some instrumental questions); the process was owned by the employees. To facilitate this deep involvement in decision making, employees often are given representation on the organization's board of directors and have stock ownership in the firm. This helps them feel and act as owners of the firm.

Organizations that embrace a high-involvement approach are relatively rare in practice. Large, public companies are a particular exception. Many leaders are uncomfortable with this more radical approach to employee involvement. And in many companies, employees do not have the wherewithal to accept this kind of involvement, whether for a lack of training or interest. Obviously, this approach is not for the faint of heart. Implementing a high-involvement approach is best done in an incremental way, beginning with the suggestion and job-involvement systems described above. Then as employees develop appropriate capabilities and managers increase their comfort level with such deep involvement, high involvement will come more naturally.

Although high-involvement systems are rare in the corporate world, they represent the kind of power sharing required by a truly empowering environment. Suggestion systems and job involvement, though worthwhile in themselves, fall short of enlisting people as partners in the business. The farther an organization travels in the direction of high involvement, the more it can capitalize on its employees' leadership capabilities.

■ Mutual Trust and Openness as a Discipline

When we work with executives, we often hear them say something like the following: "We've done all these things—given up control, built trust, freely shared information—but we still see our people acting the way they always do, resisting our efforts to share control with them and acting in disempowered ways." These comments point to an important truth. Even if we have done our best to create an environment of openness and trust, it still may be difficult for employees to take the torch and run with it, to accept that we genuinely value their exercising the control we share with them. We may hear excuses about why they can't really take on this kind of leadership, or even why they don't want to. Jim O'Toole tells the story of CEO Percy Barnevik's attempt to empower his employees at the ABB group, the global industrial, energy and automation company based in Europe:

For almost two years, people at all levels of ABB continued to try to kick important decisions back up the line. The common refrain was, "Boss, this is a tough decision; you'll have to make it." After all, why would any reasonable person want to be held accountable for a decision that might turn out to be wrong, that might be unpopular with others? . . . Hell no, let the boss decide. But Barnevik recognized that if he let his people get away with it, all decisions would end up back on his desk. If that happened, the changes needed at ABB wouldn't occur, he would be making decisions that others were more qualified to make (by virtue of their proximity to relevant information), and people at all levels would be passively standing around with no stake in making sure that decisions were implemented.[13]

Why would employees resist taking control? They may have "grown up" in a command-and-control system where they have been conditioned over time to be loyal and obedient. They may have been punished in the past for taking initiative, for trying something new. They may have made a mistake and then had to pay for it in the form of a reprimand or a lower salary increase. They may have had a boss who had the philosophy of the famous producer Samuel Goldwyn, who is reported to have said, "I want everybody to tell me the truth—even though it may cost him his job." In this kind of work environment, people learn not to trust in their own intuition and resist efforts at real employee involvement in decision making.

Part of the discipline of creating an atmosphere of trust and openness, then, is to help people unlearn their disempowerment. In part, that means communicating continuously in both word and action that we mean what we say about the leadership we expect from them. As the employees of Ralph Stayer, the CEO of Johnsonville Foods, said when he began an intense effort to share control with his people, "We thought Ralph was losing it. We didn't think he *really* wanted us to do what he was saying."

How do we overcome these kinds of beliefs? As we have emphasized throughout this book, the first step is to be consistent and avoid sending mixed messages. That means allowing people to make mistakes and helping them learn from those mistakes rather than punishing them, whether in material terms or by frowns of disapproval. Trust will evaporate quickly if our deeds don't match our words, but it takes real commitment to walk the talk.

Second, we need to model empowered behavior by acting in the way we expect others to act. In the context of this chapter, that means in part staying committed to openness and trust even when being open and trusting is discomfiting to us. This is often most difficult to do during times of crisis or decline when the natural tendency is to reclaim control and centralize resources.[14] We need to counter that tendency by not reverting to withholding information or reimposing control the first time people do something we disapprove of.

Third, we need to be sure that we are providing what people need to share control, such as relevant information and the training to interpret it.

Finally, we need to stick with the approach of sharing responsibility even if employees initially seem to resist doing their part. It means that we resist taking back control when employees express reluctance in making decisions themselves. As one executive has said, "My policy is to be sure that when people leave my office, they take their problems with them. I don't let them leave the problems on my desk."

Once people get a taste of shared control, they are likely to embrace it and say, "Why didn't we do this a long time ago? We never knew work could be this good." In his recent book, Jim O'Toole quotes the contemporary British poet Christopher Logue, who nicely captures the energy that can be released when we can help people overcome their fears:[15]

Come to the edge.
We might fall.
Come to the edge.
It's too high!
COME TO THE EDGE!
And they came
And he pushed
And they flew . . .

In your empowerment journal, reflect on what you would do in the following situation. You have encouraged a subordinate to make certain kinds of important decisions. Clearly uncomfortable with exercising his responsibility, the subordinate comes to you and asks lots of questions that, in effect, throw the decision back to you. Would you be more inclined to take over the decision yourself? If you do, what happens to the goal of nudging your subordinate toward empowerment? If not, what do you say to leave the decision with the subordinate while being sensitive to his discomfort with making it? The challenge is all about how to nudge employees to accept this kind of responsibility while giving them the kind of security and support we discussed in the last chapter.

CHAPTER SUMMARY

In this chapter, we explored one element of the second tension inherent in an empowering system—the need to create a climate of trust and openness. Doing so requires giving up control so that employees have the freedom to innovate, take initiative, and participate in meaningful business decisions.

Though it is easy to talk about giving up control, in practice managers often feel threatened by doing so. It's easier to value empowerment in ourselves than in our subordinates, and our socialization only reinforces our tendency to hang onto our control and authority.

You can share control with employees several ways. A fundamental step is to ensure that there is a free flow of real-time, critical information, including the kinds of sensitive information that in many organizations is jealously guarded. Suggestion systems and job-involvement approaches are additional steps in the direction of empowerment, but they fall short of genuinely sharing decision-making power. A high-involvement system is genuinely empowering; in a high-involvement organization, employees have considerable say not only over how to do their own jobs but how the organization will reach its strategic goals.

Employees at all levels of the organization have often been conditioned by a command-and-control bureaucracy where the primary value is obedience. Part of the discipline of creating a climate of openness and trust is helping people overcome their past learning by consistently reinforcing the message of empowerment, acting in accordance with this message, and giving people what they need to act like leaders.

The Fifth Discipline

Continuous Guidance and Control

In the early stages of our research on empowerment, we encountered a puzzling anomaly. Writings in the popular business press seemed to suggest that empowering systems had little or no structure and set few boundaries on employees' decision-making authority. An empowering system had no rules and procedures, no guidelines for action, and no hierarchy. Employees had complete freedom to do things as they saw best. Supposedly, employees would feel empowered when they could figure things out on their own. But when we conducted our research, we found that a system with little structure, few rules and procedures, and no hierarchy was *negatively* related to employee feelings of empowerment. The research not only failed to support our hypothesis about what constituted an empowering system, but actually suggested its opposite.

At first, we were perplexed by this finding. How could so many writers on empowerment be so wrong? To make sense of this anomalous finding, we went back to the people we had studied and asked them to help us interpret our findings. They had no trouble helping us understand why our finding was indeed authentic. They told us that every system needs order, otherwise people feel out of control—they experience chaos rather than freedom.

Many people share the misunderstanding implied by our initial supposition that empowering systems are places of total freedom. This misunderstanding can have devastating effects on attempts to restructure organizations in the name of "empowerment." For example, several years ago a *Fortune* 100 company went through a considerable downsizing.

The company chairman adopted an efficiency formula proposed by Charles Handy: "1/2 times 2 times 3—half as many people, being paid twice as well, working three times as hard."[1] As the downsizing was being implemented, the organization used it as an opportunity to restructure with the goal of empowering the workforce. The organizational structure was flattened. Two entire layers of hierarchy were eliminated. Many middle managers were laid off or reassigned. Employees were told that they now had authority to make significant decisions themselves. Unfortunately, most of them felt unprepared to make such decisions. In particular, they were confused about the boundaries of their decision-making authority. For example, how much money could they decide to spend without getting approval? Could they make a change in department policy without going through the usual bureaucratic process? Moreover, with formal lines of communication frayed, employees were not always sure who to report to or who to go to when they needed help. The result was intense anxiety and paralysis. Rather than feeling liberated by their freedom and autonomy, employees felt overwhelmed and lost.

This experience points to the need to balance the discipline of trust and openness with the discipline of continuous control and guidance. True, empowering systems are quite distinct from traditional command-and-control systems. As described in the preceding chapter, a command-and-control approach to management operates on the principle of centralized control. The leaders are the people at the top who set the direction and make the important decisions. Such a system is designed to minimize variation and maximize control. In contrast, an empowering system aims to increase the variation in behavior by invoking initiative on the part of employees. Instead of a single leader or a small group of leaders, it assumes that everyone can exercise leadership. It encourages self-management instead of close supervision, broad latitudes of discretion instead of narrowly constrained authority, and active participation by employees at all levels in significant decision making. But this contrast should not be understood as a contrast of polar opposites. Structure and control are not the enemies of empowerment; on the contrary, they are necessary to empowerment. The antithesis of a command-and-control approach is not empowerment but a chaotic system in which managers abdicate their role of guidance and control.

In this chapter, we explore the processes and structures that provide the control and guidance necessary for employees to feel liberated but not overwhelmed. We first consider how managers and organizations can set boundaries that channel employees' energy and autonomy into empowered action. We then consider the role of feedback in ensuring adequate guidance. Finally, we look at variations in organizational structure that provide for control and order while allowing employees ample room for empowered action.

■ Creating Empowering Boundaries

The purpose of boundaries is to provide guidance to employees about what decisions and actions are appropriate. As Ken

Blanchard has observed, "A river without banks is a large puddle."[2] Empowerment is not a formless puddle, but a powerful river whose banks are the boundaries that define employees' freedom of action.

Especially in the early stages of empowerment, when an organization is reducing the levels of hierarchy, a clear understanding of the limits of employees' decision-making authority helps reduce the disabling potential of uncertainty and ambiguity that so often accompanies this kind of change. It isn't just that the absence of clear boundaries may produce rash or ill-advised action, but also that employees might be discouraged from taking empowered action in the first place. With good reason, employees are sometimes afraid that management will say to them, "Sure, you are empowered, but not *that* empowered." Jim O'Toole provides a wonderful example of what happens when people don't understand the boundaries of their discretion.

Try to recall the first time you were given authority to do a job. Perhaps you were asked to clean out your neighbor's garage. The neighbor said, "Mary, you are now eleven and old enough to make this messy garage neat, orderly, spick-and-span. I'll be back at five o'clock to inspect your work." With youthful energy and enthusiasm, you busted your little keister to make the joint shine. As the hour of five approached, you proudly surveyed your work, expecting soon to win approval and praise (and perhaps even a bonus). So what did your neighbor probably say? "Hey, I told you to tidy the place up, but I never said anything about hosing down the floor! You didn't throw away my old *Life* magazines, did you? Why did you hide my tools where I can't find them? And who gave you permission to paint that wall?. . ." No wonder people resist taking responsibility! When leaders attempt to "empower" them, common sense tells them that nobody is ever fully empowered. There are always limits to our authority and negative consequences if we exceed those limits.[3]

So what can one do to unleash the energy and initiative within people but with appropriate direction? O'Toole gives us some clues in his account of what Percy Barnevik did at the ABB group, the global industrial, energy, and automation company based in Europe:

From day one as CEO of ABB, Barnevik recognized that the company's success depended on overcoming the natural resistance of managers to take initiative and to be held accountable. He understood that before ABB people would put themselves on the line, they needed to know exactly how much authority they had. Because his managers needed to know the boundaries of the game, Barnevik began his first meeting as leader of ABB by offering the following guidelines, which he called the General Principles of Management Behavior:

- To take action (and stick out one's neck) and do the right things is obviously best.
- To take action and do the wrong things (within reason and a limited number of times) is second best.
- Not to take action (and lose opportunities) is the only nonacceptable behavior.[4]

Barnevik's guidelines capture the spirit of empowerment, but as managers we need to go farther. Let's consider more closely what kinds of boundaries need to be set and how they should established.

What Boundaries Do We Need to Set?

By *boundaries* we mean rules that demark limits. They help employees distinguish appropriate from inappropriate behavior. They tell employees how far they can go without repercussion.

For example, most universities set a limit of one day per week on the amount of consulting faculty are allowed to do. The logic is that any more than fifty-two days per year would take away from teaching and research productivity. But within this limitation, faculty have the freedom to choose how much, when, and with whom they consult.

To set a boundary is quite different from prescribing specific courses of action. If we want people to behave like leaders, we need to allow them ample freedom in determining how best to carry out their responsibilities while still being clear about what the limits of that freedom are. Being clear about limits has two aspects: clarifying the employee's *zone of authority,* or the space in which he or she can make decisions, and clarifying the *magnitude* of the decisions the employee is free to make.

First, boundaries can specify the types of decisions employees can make. People need to know what they are responsible for and what is beyond their zone of authority. For example, when companies implement self-managing teams, the teams are told specifically that they can make decisions regarding the selection, development, and operations of their team. They might even be told that they can make decisions about new product development. But they often are told that they do not have the authority or discretion to fire team members. The organization wants its human resource staff to be involved with firing decisions because they are such a rare occurrence and because they need special handling. Furthermore, organizations often find ways to reassign problem employees to different jobs for which they might be better suited, something the team clearly is not in a position to do.

Second, boundaries can specify the magnitude of employees' decision-making discretion. For example, in the case of spending decisions, many organizations specify the amount employees can spend without getting prior approval. Clearly, some limit is needed for prudent financial control, but to allow for empowered action the limit needs to be high enough that employees can take the initiative in responding to the needs of customers, providing themselves with adequate resources, or otherwise engaging in empowered action. These kinds of boundaries send a clear message that employees are trusted to use their best discretion in creating customer satisfaction, within ample limits.

How Should We Set Boundaries?

As we remarked about vision, both the content of boundaries and the process of setting them are relevant to empowerment. Here are several considerations to take into account when setting boundaries.

First, only a few critical boundaries should be set. If an organization sets up too many boundaries, the boundaries begin to resemble policies and procedures, detailed rules that work against empowered behavior by constraining people's ability to make decisions based on circumstances and their understanding of what the organization is trying to do. For example, Disney theme parks might say they want employees to be empowered to provide excellent customer service, but they create expansive standard operating procedures that leave little room for employee discretion. Hence, almost all employee behavior is prescribed.

One question to ask is what boundaries are absolutely necessary to keep people from tripping over one another's areas of responsibility. One person's empowerment should not create chaos for someone else. This point concerns having clear, if broadly defined, zones of authority.

A second question to ask is what boundaries are necessary to protect the organization or the unit from intolerable risk. For example, there might be areas where safety is an issue (employees are not free to choose whether to wear a hardhat on a construction set or safety goggles on the production floor) or where legal issues may arise (employees or teams may not unilaterally decide to fire someone because of the potential for discrimination lawsuits).

A third question is what boundaries are necessary to protect an organization's mission, overall strategy, and core values. For example, if the vision of the Ritz-Carlton Hotel emphasizes a luxurious customer experience, the organization might want to set some boundaries on employee actions that might cheapen its image. It is not acceptable for an employee, say, to order a cheaper brand of coffee that would be obvious to the discriminating tastes of the customer, even if employees were empowered to manage their department's budget.

Second, boundaries should be wide enough to allow significant room for discretion and initiative. Boundaries that foster empowerment do not prescribe exactly what should be done; instead, they are designed to protect employees and the organization from a worst-case scenario—an employee who is a loose cannon or who literally gives the store away. Returning to the Ritz-Carlton example, the $1,500 limit on employee's discretionary spending is set high enough to give employees considerable decision-making latitude, thus allowing them to respond promptly and creatively to customers' complaints. At the same time, it signals to employees that they wouldn't want to give guests their $25,000 wedding reception for free if they complained about the sound system.

Third, managers need to ensure that employees understand the reasons for the critical boundaries that are not open to discussion. For example, if employees understand that certain constraints on their behavior are mandated by law (such as OSHA safety regulations or federal laws on employment discrimination), they will not see these boundaries as inconsistent with the message of empowerment.

Fourth, wherever possible, employees should have a say in the setting of boundaries. This is an extension of the principle that an empowering system involves employees in significant decisions. When managers decide what they think are appropriate boundaries without getting input from employees, they send a mixed message about expecting employees to display leadership. Involving employees in setting boundaries is a way of including them in the leadership conversation as well as a way of giving them a stake in the boundaries that are set.

In fact, if employees are asked what kinds of decisions and of what magnitude they are comfortable making, the chances are that they will propose boundaries that are tighter than what the managers would set themselves. For all the concern about loose cannons, especially in the early stages of empowerment, a more common concern is likely to be employees who are hesitant to act with discretion. If employees need to be nudged toward empowerment, their recommendations for relatively tight boundaries can be honored at first. As they build appropriate skills and confidence, the boundaries can gradually be loosened, again with their participation.

In your journal, list the boundaries that operate in your workplace. Do they tend to make you feel empowered or disempowered? Which ones should be better defined? Which ones should be broadened? Put yourself in the place of your direct reports—how would they answer these same questions? What boundaries are truly critical for their empowerment? Design a process for developing an optimal set of boundaries for your people.

■ Providing Empowering Feedback

Setting boundaries is one kind of essential input that enables people to be intelligently self-managing. This kind of feedback is prospective: It defines a range of appropriate action in advance. But boundaries are incomplete without constructive feedback on how employees exercise their freedom.

This point highlights another of the many misunderstandings about empowerment. Encouraging empowered self-management doesn't eliminate the need for managers to provide constructive guidance; on the contrary. To feel empowered, people need regular feedback about how they are doing. Without feedback, trying to manage and improve your own performance is like trying to improve your golf swing by hitting golf balls in the dark. Unless you see where the ball goes, you can't know whether your swing is getting any better. Similarly, without feedback on how they are exercising their initiative and discretion, people are likely to just keep doing the same things, hoping that they are the right things to be doing.

Performance feedback also reinforces a sense of accountability—that you are responsible for your results. It helps people develop their sense of competence by showing them what they do well and how they can go about working on areas that need strengthening. And it helps to focus employees' attention by sending an important signal about the company's values and priorities. It tells them what to pay attention to and what *not* to pay attention to. For example, if information on quality is measured and disseminated to employees, they will pay more attention to quality. If quality is measured but productivity is not, employees may spend a great deal of time trying to get perfect quality at the expense of productivity.

Since feedback reinforces what the organization cares about, it should be obvious that making empowered behavior a priority means ensuring that feedback is deliberately directed to aspects of empowered behavior. That means giving specific feedback on behaviors such as taking initiative, coming up with new ideas, and making the organization's priorities one's own. Some employees may need encouragement to dare more; some may need to be reminded of boundaries that they are violating. Especially in the beginning stages of an empowerment effort, employees may need considerable feedback to understand and internalize what counts as "success" in this new environment.

Ideally, feedback mechanisms should be built right into the job. Salespeople, for example, get feedback every time they make a sale or lose one. Other frontline workers do not have direct relationships with the customer, so some companies go to great lengths to see that customer complaints go directly to the involved employees. For example, complaints at a company that manufactures welding equipment go right back to the production workers who make the affected products.

In a similar way, managers can ensure that all employees—not just people in the management chain—get real-time reports on sales, costs, success in meeting production schedules, profits, or whatever information is relevant to show them the direct or indirect results of their efforts. Although this kind of immediate feedback is not possible in all types of jobs, it's worth asking what feedback mechanisms might be possible that no one has yet considered.

There is also the when and how of feedback. It is desirable for both the giver and the receiver to be able to plan ahead. Set a mutually convenient time and select an appropriate place. The setting should make both people as comfortable as possible. In terms of the process, here are some guidelines to note:

- Before giving feedback, make sure that you are not operating out of anger or other negative emotions. If you feel such emotions, take some time to work them out. If you give feedback with a negative motive, recipients will tend to shut down and not hear what you are telling them.
- In giving feedback, think of yourself as a mentor not an emperor. Get out of the expert-boss mentality. The objective is an empowering process not an abusive experience. Think through what would be open communication if you were the recipient of the feedback.
- Consult your records, review previous objectives and agreements, and make lists of specific positive and negative incidents that you feel are of consequence.

- While giving feedback, use *I* statements rather than *you* statements. Ultimately your feedback is based on your own perceptions, thoughts, and feelings. You need to own them as such.
- Be as specific as possible in describing actual behaviors. Provide illustrations of what you value and do not value. Talk about the behavior, not the person: *This action was problematic because . . .*, not *You're a problem.*
- Invite a response from the recipient, including challenge. Ask the person to clarify, explain, change, or correct. You need communication, not withdrawal. Only if you are open to learning will the recipient be open to learning.
- Clarify the boundaries. Expand and contract the boundaries as necessary so the person feels empowered. Get clear agreements. Reiterate your understanding of the agreements and ask the person also to reiterate.

The need for constructive feedback is not something we ever outgrow, no matter how well-developed our leadership abilities are. How often have you heard a top leader say, when someone does describe the consequences of the leader's actions: "Why has no one told me this before? I never would have made those decisions if I had known!" Think of the legendary isolation of U.S. presidents; many a chief executive has committed blunders for lack of timely feedback. Top executives often develop bad habits of which they may be completely unaware, and no one around them dares to give them honest feedback. One executive had the habit of constantly interrupting his people when he spoke with them. As a result, people rarely got their ideas across before the executive would sidetrack them with his interruption. And the executive compounded the problem because if anyone ever tried to tell him about this bad habit, they were quickly interrupted and sidetracked. The executive never appreciated how his behavior affected others.

Continuous and timely feedback helps ensure that empowered behavior is on track and in line with the organization's vision. Moreover, what worked yesterday may no longer be working today. As one executive said, "Success teaches all the wrong lessons." To be effective, feedback needs to be continuous as well as timely.

The essential point is that guidance in the form of performance feedback is just as important in an empowering environment as it is in a traditional management environment, if not more so. Think of feedback as an ongoing process. Identify the behaviors you care about, and then make sure that you have a way of giving continuous feedback to employees on each one. Being empowered is all about learning and growing. And the way we learn and grow is by getting feedback on the results of our actions and decisions.

 List the best and worst performance feedback sessions you have ever had. Drawing on your best experience, list the characteristics of your ideal feedback session with your boss. Ask your direct reports about what they think the characteristics are of an ideal feedback session with you. Use your own experience and your employees' input to develop a list of reminders for yourself.

■ Creating Empowering Structures

Every organization needs structures that provide a measure of order and stability and that define the formal relationships within the firm, both vertical and horizontal. The question is, what kind of organizational design meets these essential needs while freeing employees to take initiative and exercise leadership? We have found that three types of design facilitate empowerment: flatter hierarchies, wider spans of control, and team-based structures.

Flatter Hierarchies

There are endless condemnations of hierarchy in the business literature. Many people have predicted that the hierarchical organization will disappear. It has not and it will not. Hierarchy is a natural and inevitable way of increasing the efficiency of human effort.

This is an unusual statement in a book on empowerment. People who advocate empowerment almost always use hierarchy as a whipping boy. But the real issue is not hierarchy, but rather hierarchy that is excessive and dysfunctional. Here is a statement on the subject of hierarchy that every manager should consider:

> The criticism often leveled at hierarchies has nothing to do with the essential structure and function of the pyramidal model. These problems all come from one source—conflict avoidance. Hierarchies become dysfunctional when decision makers don't want to confront redundancy and incompetence and instead bury the problems in another organizational layer. Or they find it too painful to confront difficult but key people who use legitimate roles and functions in illegitimate, destructive ways. Hierarchies don't do damage to businesses any more than alcohol creates problem drinking. Structures don't create problems; people do.[5]

So in seeking to develop an empowering environment, let's not throw the baby out with the bath water. Hierarchy is not the problem. Having said this we should also be clear that the shorter the distance between the work and the final decision maker, the better. That is, flatter hierarchies are faster and more responsive than taller ones. Why? Tall hierarchies limit information flow, slow down decision making, involve too many people in approving decisions, and locate decisions farther from where the real action is. In keeping with the above quote, the more layers there are, the less likely we will see the kind of discretion and initiative that characterize a company of leaders.

For example, at a large consumer products firm, product decisions have to be approved by up to twelve layers of management. Getting twelve people to agree on just about anything is difficult. And as information moves up and down the twelve levels of the organization, sensitive issues tend to get insulated from lower levels of employees. This often means that they either have less access to important information or an increased likelihood of getting information that is inaccurate. As anyone who has every played the children's game "operator" knows, information gets less and less accurate as it is filtered from person to person. And as we know from Chapter Six, without access to accurate and full information, employees are not likely to feel very empowered. Further, any decision that has to percolate through so many layers is likely to be so watered down as to have almost no impact. The outcome will be safe solutions that require little risk but also that have little creativity.

Flatter hierarchies promote empowerment because employees no longer have to worry about getting their ideas and decisions through the politics of decision makers across many different levels. This increases their propensity to be autonomous and take initiative. In the early 1990s, a new General Electric plant was built in Puerto Rico to make surge protectors for power lines. The facility employs 172 hourly workers and just fifteen salaried advisers plus the plant manager—a total of only three layers.[6] This meant that there is only one layer of management between even the lowest-level employee and the plant manager. A conventional plant would have had twice as many layers. As a result, employees feel that they have more voice in the system. They feel more accountable because there are fewer layers of insulation between them and top management. And because they can communicate with senior management more easily, they are more comfortable with the idea of taking initiative. What is more, the plant is 20 percent more productive than its nearest company equivalent.

Wide Spans of Control

Flatter hierarchies are often accompanied by wider spans of control—that is, by a greater number of direct reports to any given manager. When spans of control are narrow, meaning that few people report to each manager, it is quite easy for managers to closely monitor employees' daily activities. But as spans of control widen, it becomes increasingly difficult for managers to observe everything that employees do. After all, they can only be in one place at a time. This doesn't mean that control is abdicated, but rather that it is shared with employees. For example, Vancom Zuid-Limburg operates a public bus system. Several years ago, the company expanded the span of control of managers to bus drivers from 1:8, the traditional design used by competitors, to 1:40. Each team of forty bus drivers feels like a mini-organization, with its own bus lines and budgeting responsibilities. With such a wide span of control, Vancom expects each individual driver to assume more responsibilities on the road. Hence, the very act of widening spans of control can encourage empowerment because the manager cannot physically be there to micromanage any longer.

Of course, there are limits to how wide the span of control can be before employees feel too disconnected. If the span becomes too wide, it will be difficult to give employees the support and security discussed in Chapter Five. As with every other aspect of empowerment, these competing tensions need to be artfully balanced.

Consider the example of Taco Bell, the Mexican fast-food chain. In the late 1980s, the company widened the spans of control of regional managers from an average of five stores to an average of twelve stores. This structural change, coupled with an increased decentralization of technology, allowed store managers to feel more autonomy in how they run their stores. The regional managers were no longer able to micromanage the stores themselves because they were only on site about once a week rather than on a daily basis. As a result, store managers felt more like owners. This loosening up of management had the added benefit of developing the competence of store managers. Since they were no longer able to depend on the management skills of the regional manager for day-to-day decision making, they had to learn how to better manage the stores themselves. This increased their confidence and developed important skills that in the past had been centralized at the regional manager level.

Eventually, restaurant managers became so autonomous that Taco Bell increased the span of control for regional managers to fifty-six stores. To help combat the possibility that restaurant managers would feel a loss of connection with such a wide span of control, Taco Bell upgraded the computer technology in the restaurants to facilitate continuous contact with the home office and the regional manager. The regional manager, while not always visible in person, did keep in touch virtually to provide the support and encouragement the restaurant managers needed on a regular basis.[7]

Team-Based Structures

Many organizations today are moving toward team-based structures. In this kind of system, teams are self-managing; they have authority to make the decisions relevant to their work, including hiring, firing, disciplining, budgeting, product development, and so on. The development of a team-based design is often accompanied by the removal of layers of hierarchy and the absorption of administrative tasks previously performed by specialists, thereby avoiding the enormous costs of having people whose sole job is to watch people who watch other people do their work.

Often, teams operate as mini-organizations that offer one-stop shopping for customers. Xerox did this when they created their customer operations group, an integration of sales, shipping, installation, service, and billing so customers can keep just one phone number on their Palm Pilot. They call this kind of team a *microenterprise unit* because it handles a complete work process, with everyone on the team having a direct line of sight to the customer.[8]

Team-based structures facilitate empowerment because employees are directly involved in important decision making. Within a set of well-specified guidelines, team members run the team as they see fit, deciding as a group the best way to get the job done. Teams substitute peer-based control for hierarchical control. They help people feel that they, not just senior management, are accountable and responsible for the operation and success of the enterprise.

Chrysler empowers its product development teams. Senior managers meet with the team leaders to sketch a vision for the vehicle and to set aggressive goals for design, performance, fuel economy, and cost. What is agreed on at this meeting forms a contract, and the team is set loose. The team members don't come back to senior management unless they encounter a major problem. If senior management were to be involved, the new vehicle would become their car, but they stay out of it, and it becomes the team's car. The team members work much harder and with more pride knowing that the resulting success or failure is their own. When disputes erupt (the door weighs twenty ounces more than specified, so twenty ounces must be found from another part, for instance), the team fights it out. The result is that Chrysler gets more innovative products at lower costs.[9]

Creating a team-based design can reduce the alienation that sometimes results from working for a large organization. It gives employees a feeling of community and a sense of partnership in the operations of the organization. Often, the team has the feel of being its own mini-organization.

However, research has also shown that there can be a dark side to teams that can be experienced as disempowering by team members. The peer pressure for performance and long work hours can be a powerful source of control over workers, but excessive control is oppressive no matter who is exercising it.[10] Barker describes a team intervention at a telecommunications manufacturing organization that felt very oppressive to team members. Team members were harder on each other than the previous command-and-control management had been. They harassed each other if they were late or had to be absent, because the team bonus was on the line. If one team member was not producing up to par because of an injury or illness, rather than pitching in to help, other team members hounded the individual to improve his performance. Such pressure can be debilitating because it is often harder to let down one's teammates than one's boss. Team members who have problems are likely to feel guilt-ridden if they don't live up to the team's expectations, particularly if the rest of the team leaves them to fend for themselves. When this happens, teams can be disempowering.

Empowering teams liberate team members to want to participate and take initiative. An empowering team environment is one in which team members support and encourage each other, not where they pressure and coerce each other. In instituting teams, therefore, organizations need to ensure that team members get adequate training in group facilitation, problem solving, and conflict management.

 Consider the kinds of structures you have in your organization. How many layers exist? Are all necessary? What is your span of control? Would your direct reports say that your span is appropriate, or does it allow for too much micromanaging? How could you transform your structures to be less constraining and more liberating?

■ Continuous Control and Guidance as a Discipline

The bottom line of this discipline is that contrary to popular belief, empowerment doesn't mean cutting people loose to fend
for themselves. Empowerment requires a delicate balancing act
involving both the trust and openness talked about in Chapter
Six and the control and guidance necessary to keep people on
track and aligned. Giving up control must be accompanied by
boundaries, feedback, and structures that provide guidance on
appropriate action. This kind of control is fluid and changes as
employees develop. Consider the analogy of learning to ride a
bike. We first give children a set of training wheels to help them
develop their confidence and build the necessary muscular
strength to pedal. With training wheels, they can focus their energy on learning to steer and getting the hang of the brakes.
Once these skills are mastered, we don't just take the wheels off,
give them a push, and let them go. We help them with the scary
transition to independent riding by steadying them until they
get the momentum and balance to move forward on their own.
Then we brush them off when they fall, encourage them to keep
trying, and hold the bike while they get back on. Finally, we establish some boundaries, like telling them to obey traffic signals,
avoid riding on busy sidewalks, and keep a sharp eye out for
cars. In short, we give them the guidance and control they need
to learn to be good riders, but our goal is gradually to transfer
control to them and then let them operate within generous
boundaries. This is the approach we need to take in fostering the
self-empowerment of employees.

The discipline of continuous control and guidance is about
deliberately assessing and adapting your own management style
to develop appropriate boundaries and provide necessary feedback, as well as creating appropriate organizational structures,
to provide the control and guidance that a company of leaders
requires. What keeps these practices from eroding into a more
traditional command-and-control system is a managerial style

that is participative and involving. Your role in developing boundaries and structures is as coach and teacher rather than as director. You can bet that your people already have a very good sense of what might be the appropriate boundaries and structures for developing their leadership potential.

 In your journal, describe a process that you could use to assess the extent to which the current way of setting boundaries, giving feedback, and organizing people in your organization or unit encourages leadership behavior.

CHAPTER SUMMARY

In this chapter, we have discussed the discipline of providing continuous guidance and control as the necessary complement to the freedom and autonomy implied by a climate of openness and trust. Giving up control does not mean abdicating control; it means sharing control with employees and guiding them sufficiently so that they can do their part responsibly. We provide appropriate guidance and control when we set clear but wide boundaries; provide constructive, timely, and targeted feedback; and organize people in ways that facilitate empowered action.

Effective boundaries specify the range of employees' responsibility and the magnitude of the decisions they are free to make. In addition, boundaries should be limited to those few, critical boundaries that are necessary for the safe and responsible functioning of the organization. They should be wide enough to permit ample freedom of action, and wherever possible employees should be involved in the process of setting them.

People do not outgrow the need for constructive feedback as they become self-empowered. On the contrary, continuous feedback enables them to learn, grow, and become increasingly self-managing. Feedback that focuses on the kinds of leadership behavior that managers expect is especially important in fostering empowerment.

Three aspects of organizational design that facilitate empowered action are flatter hierarchies, wider spans of control, and team-based structures. Structures such as these move in the direction of reducing layers of management and transferring control to employees while still maintaining the necessary degree of order.

Applying the Disciplines of Empowerment in Your Organization

I n this final chapter, let's return to the big picture and discuss how to apply the disciplines of empowerment to move your own organization in the direction of becoming a company of leaders. We first present a tool for assessing the state of the disciplines in your organization. Then we summarize suggestions for improving the areas that need strengthening if you are to unleash the power in your employees.

Worksheet 8.1 will help to reveal where your organization is strongest and weakest and consequently where to focus your efforts. Take a few minutes now to complete the assessment yourself. Later, we will suggest ways to use the assessment with other people in your organization.

■ Worksheet 8.1. Empowering Environment Assessment ■

Please think about your work situation and respond to each statement using the rating scale below. As you complete each part of the assessment, total your score for that discipline.

| 1. Strongly disagree | | 4. Agree |
| 2. Disagree | 3. Neutral | 5. Strongly agree |

Continuous Vision and Challenge

_____ 1. People have a clear idea of what the vision for our organization is; they can express the vision in their own words.

_____ 2. Our vision is real; people strive to live by it.

_____ 3. We have a vision at each level of our organization.

_____ 4. The vision for our organization evokes a sense of passion in employees.

_____ 5. People feel challenged and stretched by our organization's vision.

_____ 6. The vision of our organization creates a sense of legacy in people.

_____ 7. The vision belongs to everyone in the organization, not just top management.

_____ 8. People at many different levels and parts of our organization had input into the development of our vision statement.

_____ 9. We frequently revisit our vision statement to refresh and update it as needed.

_____ 10. Our vision reinforces the core values of our organization.

_____ Total score for vision

Continuous Support and Security

_____ 11. People can call on their colleagues at a moment's notice when help is needed.

_____ 12. People feel that the organization's top managers understand and support their needs.

_____ 13. Employees believe their job is secure.

_____ 14. People are not afraid to make mistakes; if a mistake is made, people are encouraged to find ways to develop and grow from it.

■ Worksheet 8.1. Empowering Environment Assessment, Cont'd ■

_____ 15. People feel they are rewarded for both individual achievement and significant contributions to the success of the organization.

_____ 16. People feel that they have the resources they need to do their jobs.

_____ 17. People feel that management puts people's safety first.

_____ 18. People feel buffered from change they do not need to endure.

_____ 19. People are satisfied that the training they get enables them to develop new skills to excel in their jobs.

_____ 20. People feel challenged, but they do not feel they are being overworked.

_____ Total score for support and security

Continuous Openness and Trust

_____ 21. There are few undiscussable issues or sacred cows in our organization.

_____ 22. We have a norm that information is freely shared across the organization.

_____ 23. Employees know how the organization is really performing.

_____ 24. Employees are given access to data on the company's financial performance.

_____ 25. Our organization's top managers value the ideas and contributions of people at all levels.

_____ 26. Employees trust that managers are comfortable with employees acting in empowered ways.

_____ 27. Managers involve employees in organizational decision making.

_____ 28. Managers do not feel it necessary to hoard control.

_____ 29. Managers make it clear that they want employees to express their feelings.

_____ 30. Employee involvement at our company goes beyond a suggestion system for employee input.

_____ Total score for openness and trust

■ Worksheet 8.1. Empowering Environment Assessment, Cont'd ■

Continuous Control and Guidance

_____ 31. People in our organization are clear about what is expected of them.

_____ 32. Managers in our organization provide guidance without excessive control.

_____ 33. Our spans of control do not allow for excessive micromanaging.

_____ 34. Our organization does not have unnecessary layers of management.

_____ 35. Top managers are open to feedback about their behavior.

_____ 36. Employees get clear and consistent feedback about their performance, whether directly from their job or from their manager.

_____ 37. Employee behavior is coordinated through the use of teams.

_____ 38. People have a clear sense of accountability.

_____ 39. We do a good job of measuring performance.

_____ 40. Boundaries are developed with the input of employees.

_____ Total score for control and guidance

Calculating an Overall Empowering Environment Score

Enter the scores from each of the disciplines in the appropriate space below and add the scores together for an overall score.

_____   Vision

+ _____   Support and security

+ _____   Openness and trust

+ _____   Control and guidance

_____ Overall empowering environment score

Interpreting Your Score: How Empowering Is Your Organization?

180–200	Congratulations! Your organization's environment makes it easy for people to feel empowered.
130–179	You are well on your way to creating an empowering system for your people.
100–129	You have the beginnings of an empowering system. Keep working at it.
50–99	There is lots of room for improvement. Use the ideas in this book to help your organization become more empowering.
0–49	Your system is disempowering to people. Now is the time to change.

Are you satisfied with your overall empowerment score? Why or why not? If not, as a starting point, target where you have most room for improvement. On which discipline do you score lowest? Are there specific questions that you score low on, or are you low across the board on that discipline? What can you do to improve your score on that discipline? We will further address this last question in the following sections.

■ Using the Assessment as an Exercise in Empowerment

Taking this assessment is only a first step in understanding your organization. A self-assessment provides only a limited, one-sided evaluation of your environment. It is sometimes easy for us to mislead ourselves in self-assessments. Ideally, to get a more accurate and complete picture of your organization, have everyone in your organization (or your own direct reports at a minimum) complete the assessment. Only when you have a range of people complete the assessment can you have a real sense for how your people are experiencing their workplace.

It is important they can complete the assessment anonymously so they can be completely honest. However, you may want to consider having respondents identify their unit, department, job level, and job type so you make some comparisons, but this may increase concerns about anonymity. Have respondents put their completed assessment into an unmarked envelope that they can drop into a box at their convenience.

Once your deadline for completed assessments has passed, compile the information from across the assessments. This could be done by you, or ideally by a group of your people to encourage complete involvement. Compute an average score across all completed assessments for each question as well as for each overall discipline. If you collected information on job type, level, unit, or department, you could also examine any patterns across the different groups.

Then bring together everyone you asked to complete the assessment to discuss the findings. Provide the actual numbers to the group. A careful analysis of average scores could suggest where empowerment efforts are succeeding the most (where the highest scores are found) and where they are succeeding least (where the lowest scores are found). Rather than giving your own interpretations of what you see in the results, give others a chance to give their viewpoints first. Once you have collected the interpretations of what the findings mean, discuss what action steps might make sense. This discussion might be saved for a second meeting so that people have time to absorb the findings. Groups of like employees may want to work together to develop action proposals for their own departments or units.

This process often involves intense exchange. Instead of fearing such exchange, encourage it. Such discussion will tell you more about what is really going on in your organization than almost anything else you do. It also facilitates the actual process of empowerment. Because this kind of dialogue is difficult to facilitate in your position as a manager, we recommend that you bring in an external facilitator. You will find that this investment will bring a large return.

In this way the assessment might itself become an instrument of organizational change. Having others complete assessment takes courage, because the very act of assessment creates some expectation for action. The very act of completing the assessment alerts employees to potential deficiencies in your system. If you ask your people to take the time and have the courage to be honest themselves, you must respond by allowing them to see the results and by responding to areas highlighted as problematic. This kind of participative process can be empowering in and of itself.

And of course the assessment should be re-administered periodically to assess progress. It might be used in conjunction with a semiannual employee attitude survey to monitor the pulse of the organization or as part of the organization's regular strategic planning process.

In your empowerment journal, map out how you can use the assessment as an exercise in empowerment. How will you involve people in the assessment? Who can help you design the process? Who can assist you as a facilitator?

■ Building a More Empowering Environment

Perhaps you aren't satisfied with the extent to which your organization is putting the disciplines of empowerment into practice. Perhaps you work for one of the majority of organizations that have plenty of work to do when it comes to creating a genuinely empowering environment. The next step is to formulate an action plan. You can find ideas for specific steps to take in the chapters corresponding to the disciplines you want to focus on. This section summarizes some of the steps you and your colleagues and employees may want to consider. Pay particular attention to the discipline or disciplines that your assessment shows has the most room for improvement.

Continuous Vision and Challenge
1. *Develop a vision.* Work with the people in your organization to develop a clear direction for the organization. Involve people in this process. The vision belongs to everyone in the organization, not just top management. Challenge them to create a vision that is truly inspiring—one that embraces challenge, that they can be passionate about, and that creates a sense of legacy.
2. *Live the vision.* Ensure that people have a clear idea of what the vision is. Make the vision authentic by acting in ways that bring it to life. Avoid sending mixed messages about what the priorities are.

3. *Cascade the vision throughout the organization.* Develop a vision at each level of your organization that aligns with the overall organizational vision but meets the specific needs of the individual unit.
4. *Make the vision dynamic.* Revisit your vision statements regularly to refresh and update them as needed. Encourage a bottom-up process that can be initiated by anyone at any level.
5. *Challenge and stretch.* Create opportunities for people to develop and grow continually. Develop stretch objectives for people. Push them to reach higher and higher.

Continuous Support and Security
1. *Develop networks of support.* Create communities of practice where people have resources available to help them with problems as needed. Encourage friendships to develop in the workplace through the use of extracurricular activities such as sports teams, cultural events, and off-site retreats.
2. *Provide secure jobs.* Ensure employees that efficiency gains or creative ideas will not put people's jobs at risk. Help create a family atmosphere where layoffs are used as a final resort. Ensure that people receive the right kind of training to keep them highly employable.
3. *Encourage risk taking.* When mistakes are made, focus on fixing the problem and helping people learn from the mistake rather than looking for someone to blame.
4. *Keep work hours reasonable.* Avoid excessive overtime, particularly forced overtime. Make sure you have the human resources that are necessary for the amount of work that needs to be done.
5. *Train, train, train.* Give people the training they need to be self-managing. Make a commitment to invest in keeping employees' skills up-to-date.
6. *Reward for performance.* Create a pay system that pays people based on their achievement. Make sure they benefit when

the organization does well and when they meet their personal objectives. Help ensure that it is in people's best interest to improve the performance of the organization.

7. *Put safety first.* Do a safety audit. Make changes that ensure physical safety. Let people know that safety is a key value.

8. *Make sure that people have the resources they need.* Do an audit of the resources people need but cannot access. Develop systems that make such resources available.

9. *Buffer people from unnecessary change.* Don't make change just for the sake of change or just because everyone else is doing it. Change when it makes strategic sense from a business perspective.

Continuous Openness and Trust

1. *Set the tone.* Create an organizational culture that values the contributions of people at all levels. Do not tolerate managers who don't share these values. Respond quickly and publicly to actions that go against these values.

2. *Share information freely.* Ensure that there are no sacred issues at your company that can't be discussed. Create a norm of sharing information freely across the organization. Employees should have an accurate sense of how the organization is performing. They should understand basic financial analysis and what it takes to make good business decisions.

3. *Treat employees as business partners.* Involve employees in organizational decision making. Share control when possible. Make it clear that managers want employees to act in empowered ways. Make sure that employee involvement goes beyond a suggestion system for employee input.

4. *Build trust.* Show concern for the needs of your people. Don't just assume you know what their needs are—ask! Be reliable: Work to make sure your actions are consistent with your words.

Continuous Control and Guidance

1. *Make expectations clear.* Develop clear boundaries with the input of employees. Help people understand the reasons for any boundaries they do not set themselves.

2. *Evaluate and reevaluate boundaries.* Assess boundaries in terms of their number (aim for the smallest number consistent with safeguarding critical organizational interests) and breadth (as wide as possible to allow for empowered action). Loosen boundaries as employees grow in their ability to use discretion wisely.

3. *Create empowering structures.* Flatten hierarchies; get by with the fewest layers of management as possible. Make sure that lines of authority are clear and that people have a clear understanding of their tasks and responsibilities. Develop wide spans of control that inhibit micromanaging. Where possible, make use of teams.

4. *Develop accountability.* Make sure that people have a clear sense of their responsibility to the organization. Measure performance so that people know how well they are doing. Provide constructive feedback on a regular basis.

■ Are There Some People Who Don't Want to Be Empowered?

As you consider ways to make your organizational environment more empowering, you may find yourself confronting a fundamental issue: Does everyone really want to be empowered? And what do I do if they don't?

Our experience is that when an organization begins an effort to empower its workforce, employees may respond in a variety of ways. Let's consider what you might do in each case, beginning with employees whose first response is basically positive.

- "We're already there." A number of your people already feel and behave in empowered ways. They will be advocates for your empowerment efforts because they are probably frustrated that others do not take initiative and feel the sense of ownership they do. These will be people you can draw on to help win over potential critics. Use them to your advantage. Involve them early and have them help you strategize to overcome possible barriers.

- "We're interested." A sizable portion of your people will probably be favorable to the notion of empowerment and will embrace the effort. So before you even begin, almost half of your workforce will be favorably disposed. It is important that their initial experiences are positive. Use employees who are already empowered to mentor and assist others.

Another proportion of your workforce will be more of a challenge. They may respond in one of the following ways:

- "We're not too sure about this." Some employees may be on the fence. Typically, these folks have been born and bred in a command-and-control system. They have been conditioned to be obedient and follow orders. Empowered behaviors will not come naturally to them. Some people may be unsure because they have been exposed to prior change efforts that didn't work. And some people who are nearing retirement may hope they can hold off change for a couple years to get to the promised land. With employees who "aren't sure about this," the challenge is to build trust that it is in their interest to be empowered and help them build the confidence necessary to act in empowered ways. Keep in mind that trust and confidence cannot be developed overnight. What happens with others will affect this group; they will be watching those who expressed interest to see whether management is really putting its money where its mouth is.

- "We get our fulfillment elsewhere." Another part of your workforce may not want a job that involves empowerment. They may prefer to get fulfillment from other aspects of life, such as their family, church, or volunteer activities. They may want a job where they only have to follow directions in order to get paid. Sometimes, these people can be inspired by a compelling vision of the future in the organization. In certain cases, there may be a job in your organization where this kind of employee will thrive and where empowerment is unnecessary, but these jobs are likely to be few. If you move toward demanding a high degree of empowerment, some individuals may need to be encouraged to find employment elsewhere in a more command-and-control-oriented environment.

- "You've got to be kidding." A few people may have such an adversarial relationship with the organization that they cannot be open-minded enough to understand the need for empowerment. With extreme efforts, many of these people can be turned around, but there may be some diehards who simply won't change. In these rare cases, it may be necessary to let the employee go rather than allow one bad seed to infect the rest of the workforce. However, this should only be done as a last resort, and the reasons for doing so should be carefully communicated to the rest of the workforce.

In only a few organizations do we find that all employees are empowered. It is not necessary or likely that every single person will be empowered. If you can even get 10 percent of your people to empower themselves, the impact will be significant. The effect is likely to be contagious to the rest of your workforce. The initial few who are empowered will attract more people who, in turn, will empower themselves. The point here is not to expect everyone to respond to your change efforts in the same way. Be prepared for a range of responses, and plan in advance what to do to develop the readiness of your workforce for empowered action.

 As a final journal exercise, think about who in your organization might fit into each of these groups. Consider two actions that you can take with each group to minimize their potential for resistance.

CHAPTER SUMMARY

If you are committed to improving your organization's performance with respect to the disciplines of empowerment, begin with assessing where you already are. The assessment instrument provided in this chapter can help you identify specific areas on which to focus. Going beyond self-assessment can give you a more complete picture of your organization. An assessment that draws on the broad involvement of your organization can be used as a stimulus for real organizational change. Focus on the areas that most need improvement, and be sure to reassess how the organization is doing on a regular basis. Don't take success for granted; performance can deteriorate as well as improve over time.

Once you assess where you are now, the next step is to develop an action plan. We have provided a number of ideas in this book you can use or adapt to suit your circumstances. Commit to the plan, establish goals you can measure, and remember to allow enough time for changes to take effect. Keep the idea of discipline in mind. Setbacks are to be expected. Don't let yourself be discouraged. Stay committed to your goals. And don't forget that each discipline has its complement. To create an empowering environment is to manage the tensions of competing disciplines.

Be prepared for a range of responses to organizational change. Plan in advance how you will work with those who are unsure about empowerment or resist empowering themselves.

Finally, always keep in mind the first discipline of empowerment: Begin with yourself. Only empowered leaders can develop an empowered workforce. Only when you have begun to live empowerment does it make sense to try to foster the environmental factors that encourage others to empower themselves. At the same time, never underestimate the importance of context in influencing your own behavior and that of others. Empowerment requires attention to both the self and the surrounding environment.

In this book we have provided the keys to becoming an empowered leader and creating an empowering context. The example of a number of companies shows that putting the disciplines of empowerment into practice is the way to unleash the power in your workforce. We wish you great success as you work to create a company of leaders.

Notes

Chapter One

1. Adapted from Robert Quinn, *Change the World: How Ordinary People Can Achieve Extraordinary Results.* San Francisco: Jossey-Bass, 2000, pp. 49–50.
2. Peter Kizilos, "Crazy About Empowerment," *Training,* December 1990, 47–56.
3. John J. Shermerhorn, Jerry G. Hunt, and Richard N. Osborne, *Organizational Behavior* (7th ed.). New York: Wiley, 2000, p. 320.
4. S. McCartney, "Control Issues: How Pilots Fly the Plane Varies a Lot from Airline to Airline," *The Wall Street Journal,* March 14, 2000, p. A1.
5. Anonymous, "Always Consult Your Employees—Even If You Don't Want To," *Fortune,* December 6, 1999, p. 320.
6. G. Imperator, "Their Specialty: Teamwork," *Fast Company,* Jan.-Feb. 2000, *31,* p. 56.
7. Gretchen M. Spreitzer, "An Empirical Test of a Comprehensive Model of Intrapersonal Empowerment in the Workplace," *American Journal of Community Psychology,* 1995, *23*(5), 601–629.
8. Aneil K. Mishra and Gretchen M. Spreitzer, "Explaining How Survivors Respond to Downsizing: The Roles of Trust, Empowerment, Justice,

and Work Redesign," *Academy of Management Review,* 1998, *23*(3), 567–588.

9. Gretchen M. Spreitzer, "Psychological Empowerment in the Workplace: Dimensions, Measurement, and Validation," *Academy of Management Journal,* 1995, *38*(5), 1442–1465.

10. Gretchen M. Spreitzer, Suzanne C. DeJanasz, and Robert E. Quinn, "Empowered to Lead: The Role of Psychological Empowerment in Leadership," *Journal of Organizational Behavior,* 1999, *20,* 511–526.

11. Gretchen M. Spreitzer and Robert E. Quinn, "Empowering Middle Managers to Be Transformational Leaders," *Journal of Applied Behavioral Science,* 1996, *32*(3), 237–261.

12. Gretchen M. Spreitzer, Suzanne C. DeJanasz, and Robert E. Quinn, "Empowered to Lead: The Role of Psychological Empowerment in Leadership," *Journal of Organizational Behavior,* 1999, *20,* 511–526.

13. Gretchen M. Spreitzer, Mark A. Kizilos, and Stephen W. Nason, "A Dimensional Analysis of the Relationship Between Psychological Empowerment and Effectiveness, Satisfaction, and Strain," *Journal of Management,* 1997, *23*(5), 679–704.

Chapter Two

1. David Dorsey, "Change Factory," *Fast Company, 35,* p. 210.

2. Suzy Wetlauer, "Organizing for Empowerment, an Interview with AES's Roger Sant and Dennis Bakke," *Harvard Business Review,* 1999, *77*(1), 112.

3. Suzy Wetlauer, "Organizing for Empowerment, an Interview with AES's Roger Sant and Dennis Bakke," p. 112.

4. Robert E. Quinn and Gretchen M. Spreitzer, "The Road to Empowerment: Seven Questions Every Leader Should Consider," *Organizational Dynamics,* Autumn 1977, *26*(2), 38–39.

Chapter Three

1. Kenneth H. Blanchard, *The Heart of a Leader: Insights on the Art of Influence.* Tulsa, Okla.: Honor Books, 1999, p. 152.

2. Robert E. Quinn, *Deep Change: Discovering the Leader Within.* San Francisco: Jossey-Bass, 1996, pp. 31–32.

3. Joseph Campbell, *The Hero with a Thousand Faces.* New York: World Publishing, 1968.
4. Robert E. Quinn, Gretchen M. Spreitzer, and Matthew V. Brown, "Changing Others Through Changing Ourselves: The Transformation of Human Systems," *Journal of Management Inquiry,* 2000, *9,* 157–158.
5. Kenneth H. Blanchard, *The Heart of a Leader: Insights on the Art of Influence.* Tulsa, Okla.: Honor Books, 1999, p. 156.
6. R. Leider, "Don't You Get It?" *Fast Company,* June 2000.
7. James O'Toole, *Leadership A to Z: A Guide for the Appropriately Ambitious.* San Francisco: Jossey-Bass, 1999.
8. James M. Kouzes and Barry Z. Posner, "Bringing Leadership Lessons from the Past into the Future," in W. Bennis, G. Spreitzer, and T. Cummings (eds.), *The Future of Leadership: Today's Top Thinkers Speak to the Next Generation.* San Francisco: Jossey-Bass, 2001.

Chapter Four

1. Noel Tichy and Stratford Sherman, *Control Your Destiny or Someone Else Will: How Jack Welch Is Making General Electric the World's Most Competitive Corporation.* New York: Currency Doubleday, 1993.
2. L. E. Fisher, *Gandhi.* New York: Simon & Schuster, 1995. Quote can be found on the MK Gandhi Institute for Non-Violence Website: http://www.gandhiinstitute.org.
3. Gary Hamel and C. K. Prahalad, *Competing for the Future.* Boston: Harvard Business School Press, 1994.
4. "The Top 25 Managers of the Year," *Business Week,* January 8, 2000, pp. 60–80.

Chapter Five

1. E. Neuborne and R. Berner, "Warm and Fuzzy Won't Save Procter & Gamble," *Business Week,* June 2000, *26,* 48.
2. David Whetten, "What Really Matters," presidential address to the meeting of the National Academy of Management, August 6, 2000.
3. Karen Mishra, Gretchen M. Spreitzer, and Aneil Mishra, "Preserving Employee Morale During Downsizing," *Sloan Management Review,* Winter 1998, *39*(2), 83–95.

4. J. Pfeffer and J. F. Viega, "Putting People First for Organizational Success," *The Academy of Management Executive,* 1999, *13*(2), 37–48.

5. http://www.arthurandersen.com/website.nsf/content/NorthAmerica UnitedStatesCareersFortune100Flash?OpenDocument.

6. Robert Levering and Milton Moskowitz, "The Best 100 Companies to Work For," *Fortune,* January 8, 2001, pp. 149–168.

7. E. O. Welles, "Motherhood, Apple Pie, and Stock Options," *Inc. Magazine,* February 1998, pp. 84–97.

Chapter Six

1. Jeffrey Pfeffer and John F. Viega, "Putting People First for Organizational Success," *The Academy of Management Executive,* 1999, *13*(2), 37–48.

2. James O'Toole, *Leadership from A to Z: A Guide for the Appropriately Ambitious,* p. 210.

3. M. J. Roberts, "The Johnsonville Sausage Co.," Harvard Business School Case 9–387–103, 1986.

4. Thomas A. Stewart, "Making Decisions in Real Time," *Fortune,* June 26, 2000, p. 332.

5. Aneil K. Mishra, "Organizational Responses to Crisis: The Centrality of Trust," in *Trust in Organizations: Frontiers of Theory and Research,* [pp. 261–287]. Thousand Oaks, Calif.: Sage, 1996.

6. Morgan W. McCall, Michael M. Lombardo, and Ann Lombardo, *The Lessons of Experience: How Successful Executives Develop on the Job.* New York: Lexington Books, 1990.

7. C. Michael Thompson, *The Congruent Life: Following the Inward Path to Fulfilling Work and Inspiring Leadership.* San Francisco: Jossey-Bass, 2000, p.182.

8. Jeffrey Pfeffer, *Competitive Advantage Through People: Unleashing the Power of the Workforce.* Cambridge, Mass.: Harvard Business School Press, 1996.

9. Charles Handy, *Waiting for the Mountain to Move: Reflections on Work and Life.* San Francisco: Jossey-Bass, 1999, p. 94

10. Edward E. Lawler suggested these three groups of employment involvement strategies in his "Choosing an Involvement Strategy," *The Academy of Management Executive,* 1988, *2*(3), 197–204.

11. James O'Toole, *Leadership from A to Z: A Guide for the Appropriately Ambitious,* p. 210.

12. M. J. Roberts, "The Johnsonville Sausage Co.," Harvard Business School Case, 9–387–103, 1986.

13. James O'Toole, *Leadership from A to Z: A Guide for the Appropriately Ambitious,* p. 12.

14. Barry Staw, Lance Sandelands, and Jane Dutton, "Threat Rigidity Effects in Organizational Behavior: A Multilevel Analysis," *Administrative Science Quarterly,* 1981, *26,* 501–524.

15. James O'Toole, *Leadership from A to Z: A Guide for the Appropriately Ambitious,* p. 12.

Chapter Seven

1. Charles Handy, *Waiting for the Mountain to Move: Reflections on Work and Life,* p. 113.

2. Kenneth H. Blanchard, *The Heart of a Leader: Insights on the Art of Influence,* p. 86.

3. James O'Toole, *Leadership A to Z: A Guide for the Appropriately Ambitious,* p. 11.

4. James O'Toole, *Leadership A to Z: A Guide for the Appropriately Ambitious,* p. 11.

5. Morris R. Shechtman, *Working Without a Net: How to Survive and Thrive in Today's High Risk Business World.* New York: Pocket Books Business, 1994, p. 93.

6. Thomas Stewart, "The Search for the Organization of Tomorrow," *Fortune,* May 18, 1992, pp. 92–98.

7. Leonard Schlesinger and Dena Votronbek, "Taco Bell," Harvard Business School Case 9-694-076, 1994.

8. Thomas Stewart, "The Search for the Organization of Tomorrow," p. 97.

9. Marshall Loeb, "Empowerment that Pays Off," *Fortune,* March 20, 1995, pp. 145–146.

10. James R. Barker, "Tightening the Iron Cage: Concertive Control in Self-Managing Teams," *Administrative Science Quarterly,* 1993, *38,* 408–437.

The Authors

Gretchen M. Spreitzer is an associate professor of management and organization at the Marshall School of Business at University of Southern California, where she is a faculty affiliate of both the Center for Effective Organizations and the Leadership Institute. She works in the areas of organizational behavior and human resource management, focusing her research in employee empowerment and managerial development, particularly within a context of organizational change and decline.

She has edited two books, including *The Future of Leadership: Today's Top Thinkers on Leadership Speak to the Next Generation* (with Warren Bennis and Thomas Cummings, Jossey-Bass, 2001) and *The Leader's Change Handbook: An Essential Guide to Setting Direction and Taking Action* (with Jay Conger and Edward Lawler, Jossey-Bass, 1999). Her research has been published in a number of journals, including the *Academy of Management Journal, Academy of Management Review, Industrial and Labor Relations Review, Journal of Applied Psychology, Journal of Management, Journal of Organizational Behavior, Organizational Dynamics,* and *Sloan Management Review.*

Spreitzer was also awarded the Western Academy of Management's Ascendant Scholar award for early career contributions. She is on the editorial boards of the *Journal of Organizational Behavior* and the *Journal of Management Inquiry* and serves as a reviewer for numerous journals. She is active in the National Academy of Management and the Western Academy of Management, where she holds executive positions.

Spreitzer teaches on the topics of organizational behavior, leadership, and organizational change in the MBA, undergraduate, PhD, and executive program at the Marshall School of Business and in executive programs at the Michigan Business School.

In 1992, she earned her PhD in organizational behavior from the University of Michigan Business School. She has a BS in systems analysis (1987) from Miami University, Oxford, Ohio. Prior to her graduate work, she was employed with Price Waterhouse's Government Services Office and with Partner for Livable Places, a not-for-profit urban planning firm in Washington, D.C.

Robert E. Quinn holds the M.E. Tracy Collegiate Professorship at the University of Michigan and is a professor of organizational behavior at the University of Michigan Business School. His area of research is leadership and organizational change. He has published numerous papers and books.

His most recent books are *Change the World: How Ordinary People Can Accomplish Extraordinary Results* (Jossey-Bass, 2000); *Pressing Problems in Modern Organizations* (with Lynda St. Clair and Regina O'Neill, American Management Association, 1999); and *Deep Change: Discovering the Leader Within* (Jossey-Bass, 1997). He is also the editor of the new University of Michigan Business School Management Series: Innovative Solutions to the Pressing Problems of Business, of which this book is a part.

Quinn is a founding partner of the Wholonics Leadership Group and has twenty-five years of experience in working with companies on issues of personal and organizational change.

Index